CONSIDER
THE ISSUES

CONSIDER THE ISSUES

Listening and Critical Thinking Skills

THIRD EDITION

CAROL NUMRICH

In Cooperation with NPR®

longman.com

Consider the Issues: Listening and Critical Thinking Skills, Third Edition

Pearson Education, 10 Bank Street, White Plains, NY 10606

Vice president, multimedia and skills: Sherry Preiss
Acquisitions editor: Virginia L. Blanford
Development editors: Andrea Bryant, Mykan White
Production editor: Sasha Kintzler
Art director: Elizabeth Carlson
Vice president, U.S. marketing: Kate McLoughlin
Vice president, international marketing: Bruno Paul
Senior manufacturing buyer: Nancy Flaggman
Photo research: Tara Maldonado
Cover design: Ann France
Text design: Patrice Sheridan
Digital layout specialist: Warren Fischbach

Photo Credits: p. 1, ©Rob Lewine/CORBIS; p. 16, ©Mark Richards/PhotoEdit –All rights reserved.;
p. 30 ©Telepress/CORBIS SYGMA; p. 44, ©DNA Plant Technology Corporation; p. 57, ©Elyse Lewin/Getty Images;
p. 72, ©1991 Benetton Group SpA. Photo: O. Toscani; p. 85, top: ©1991 Benetton Group SpA. Photo: O. Toscani;
middle: ©1989 Benetton Group SpA. Photo: O. Toscani; bottom: ©1992 Benetton Group SpA. Photo: Simona
Cali'Cocuzza/Black Star. Concept: O. Toscani; p. 86, top: ©1992 Benetton Group SpA. Photo: Patrick Robert/Sygma.
Concept: O. Toscani, middle: ©1996 Benetton Group SpA. Photo: O. Toscani; bottom: ©1992 Benetton Group SpA.
Photo: Lucinda Devlin. Concept: O. Toscani; p. 87, ©AFP/CORBIS; p. 103, ©Paul Avis/Taxi/Getty Images; p. 117,
©J. Pratt/The Image Works; p. 133, left: ©Yang Liu/CORBIS, middle: ©Michael Newman/PhotoEdit, right:
©Stephen Simpson/Getty Images; p. 146, ©AP Photo/Stuart Ramson; p. 159, ©David Young-Wolff/Photo Edit
Art Credits: p. 67, Lloyd P. Birmingham; p. 120, Pearson Longman

ISBN: 0-13-111593-6

Printed in the United States of America
1 2 3 4 5 6 7 8 9 10–VHG–08 07 06 05 04

CONTENTS

SCOPE AND SEQUENCE

USAGE	PRONUNCIATION	INTERACTIVE PROCESSING ACTIVITIES
Separable Phrasal Verbs	Word Stress in Separable Phrasal Verbs	Survey: Cell Phone Courtesy
Present Perfect, Present Perfect Progressive, and Simple Past	Stress Changes with the *a*-Prefix	Debate: Smoking in Public Places
Modal Perfects	Reductions of *Have*	Debate: Interviewing Children in the Media
Restrictive Adjective Clauses	Listing Intonation	Values Clarification: Genetic Experimentation
Adverbial Clauses of Contrast	/i/ and /I/	Interview: Working at Home
Descriptive Adjectives	Thought Groups	Values Clarification: Magazine Advertisements
Past Unreal Conditional	Word Stress for Meaning Differentiation	Values Clarification: The Values of a Philanthropist
Present Unreal vs. Future Unreal Conditions	Noun Compounds	Case Study: Dial-a-Doc
Present Perfect vs. Simple Past to Express Past Time	Rising Intonation	Role Play: The Courtroom
Present Unreal Conditional	Suffix Pronunciation in Different Word Forms	Survey: What Constitutes a Family?
Expressing Partial Agreement or Reservation	Stress Changes in Words with Suffixes	Simulation Game: The Daimler-Chrysler Merger
Causative Verbs	Words with Silent Consonants	Values Clarification: To Save the Earth

INTRODUCTION

Consider the Issues: Listening and Critical Thinking Skills consists of twelve authentic radio interviews and reports from National Public Radio. The broadcasts were taken from *All Things Considered, Weekend All Things Considered, Living on Earth,* and *Morning Edition.*

Designed for high-intermediate or advanced students of English as a second language, the text presents an integrated approach to developing listening comprehension and critical thinking skills. By using material produced for the native speaker, the listening selections provide content that is interesting, relevant, and educational. At the same time, nonnative speakers are exposed to unedited language, including the hesitations, redundancies, changes in speed, and various dialectal patterns that occur in everyday speech.

Each unit presents either an interview or a report about a controversial issue of international appeal. The students gain an understanding of American values, attitudes, and culture as they develop their listening skills. Throughout each unit, students are encouraged to use the language and concepts presented in the listening selection and to reevaluate their point of view.

The third edition of *Consider the Issues* offers six new units based on broadcasts about compelling contemporary topics. In addition, two sections have been expanded. *Listening* now includes a *Listening for Inference* exercise, a critical skill for mastering comprehension of authentic language. *Looking at Language* now has two parts: *Usage,* which is grammar-based, and *Pronunciation.*

SUGGESTIONS FOR USE

The exercises are designed to stimulate an interest in the material by drawing on students' previous knowledge and opinions, and by aiding comprehension through vocabulary and guided listening exercises. In a variety of discussion activities, the students integrate new information and concepts with previously held opinions.

I. Anticipating the Issue

Predicting: In this two to three minute introduction, students are asked to read the title of the interview or report and predict the content of the unit. Some of the titles require an understanding of vocabulary or idiomatic expressions that the teacher may want to explain to the students. The ideas generated by the students could be written on the chalkboard. The teacher can present this as a brainstorming activity, encouraging students to say as many ideas as they have as quickly as they can. Once the students have listened to the interview or report, they can then verify their predictions.

Thinking Ahead: Before listening to the audio, students are asked to discuss the issues to be presented in the interview or report. In groups of four or five, the students discuss their answers to general questions or react to statements that include ideas from the broadcast. The students draw on their own knowledge or experience for this exercise. It is likely that students will have different opinions, and the discussion, especially with a verbal class, could become quite lengthy. It is recommended that the teacher limit this discussion to ten or fifteen minutes, so as not to exhaust the subject prior to the listening exercises.

The teacher should also be aware that some students may be sensitive about some of the material discussed. The teacher should stress to students that there is room for all opinions, but at the same time, they should not feel compelled to talk about something that may make them feel uncomfortable.

II. Vocabulary

In this section, a variety of exercises is presented to prepare the students for vocabulary and expressions used in the listening selection.

Vocabulary in a reading passage. Vocabulary is presented in a reading passage that also introduces some of the ideas from the broadcast and provides some background information. The students should read through the text once for global comprehension. Then, as they reread the text, they match the vocabulary items with definitions or synonyms. The meaning of the new words may be derived from context clues, from general knowledge of the language, or from the dictionary.

Vocabulary in sentences. Vocabulary is presented in sentences that relate to the ideas in the listening selection. Context clues are provided in each sentence. The students should first try to guess the meaning of these words by supplying their own definition or another word that they think has a similar meaning. Although the students may not be sure of the exact meaning, they should be encouraged to guess. This will lead them to a better understanding of the new words. Once they have tried to determine the meaning of these words through context, they match the words with definitions or synonyms.

Vocabulary in word groups. Vocabulary items from the selection are presented as part of a word group. The focus is on the relationship between the vocabulary items and other words. A set of three words follows a given vocabulary item; in each set, two words have a similar meaning to the vocabulary item. It is suggested that students work together to discuss what they know about these words. Through these discussions, they will begin to recognize roots and prefixes and how these words relate to each other. The students should be encouraged to use their dictionaries for this exercise.

Vocabulary in context. Vocabulary is presented in short monologues or dialogues that are related to the ideas in the listening selection. The vocabulary item is contained in the text. With the help of context clues, students choose the continuing line of speech. To do this, they must understand the content of the monologue or dialogue as well as the meaning of the new word or phrase.

III. Listening

Task Listening: Students will now hear the listening selection for the first time. This exercise presents the students with a targeted comprehension task before asking them to focus on main ideas and details. The "task" is purposely simple; students listen for a specific piece of information in the recorded material while listening globally. Consequently, most of the students should be able to answer the questions after the first listening.

Listening for Main Ideas: The second time students hear the broadcast, they focus on the main ideas. Each interview or report has between three and five main ideas used to divide the selection into parts. Each part is introduced by a beep on the audio. Only one listening is usually required for *Listening for Main Ideas*; however, some classes may need to listen twice in order to capture the important information.

In some units, students simply answer multiple-choice questions. In other units, they are given questions or key words to guide them in comprehending the main ideas of the listening selection. In these exercises, the students are asked to write complete statements of the main ideas. The teacher should stop the audio at the sound of the beep to allow the students time to write. Students may then compare their statements to see whether they have understood the relevant information. The teacher may want to ask individual students to write the ideas on the chalkboard. From these statements, the class can discuss the ones that represent the best expression of the main points. Teachers may also ask why incorrect answers do not represent main ideas.

Listening for Details: In the third listening, the students are asked to focus on detailed information. They are first asked to read through the questions of one part. The teacher should clarify any items that the students do not understand. Then each part of the broadcast is played. The teacher should stop the audio at the sound of the beep to allow the students time to write. The students either complete missing information in sentences or answer true/false or multiple-choice questions as they listen, thus evaluating their comprehension. Finally, in pairs, they compare answers. The teacher should encourage the students to defend their answers based on their comprehension. Students should also be encouraged to use the language from the audio to convince other students of the accuracy of their answers. There will certainly be disagreements over some of the answers; the discussions will help focus attention on the information needed to answer the questions correctly. By listening to each part another time, the students generally recognize this information. Once again, they should be asked to agree on their answers. If there are still misunderstandings, the audio should be played a third time, with the teacher verifying the answers and pointing out where the information is heard on the audio.

Listening for Inference: The final listening activity focuses on inference. Students listen to different segments from the broadcast and are asked to infer or interpret the attitudes, feelings, points of view, or intended meanings expressed. To do this, they focus on speakers' tone of voice, stress and intonation patterns, and choice of language. Students may express slightly varied interpretations in their answers. This is to be expected, since inference can be subjective. This difference in interpretation can be a starting point to an interesting discussion. For this reason, there are *suggested answers* in the Answer Key.

IV. Looking at Language

Usage: In this exercise, a specific use of language from the listening selection is presented in isolation, as a further aid to comprehension. A wide variety of grammatical, semantic, and functional points are presented. The *Scope and Sequence* on pages vi–vii lists the usage points from the twelve units. Students are asked to listen to an example from the listening selection and to focus on this use of language in context. Then, through discussions and exercises, the students practice the language in a different context. These exercises are not meant to be exhaustive but rather to make students aware of a particular grammar point. The teacher may want to supplement this exercise with material from a grammar-based text.

Pronunciation: Like *Usage*, *Pronunciation* focuses on segments from the broadcast that present particular points critical to listening comprehension. Examples of intonation, stress and rhythm, and pronunciation are presented in isolation, as a further aid to comprehension. The *Scope and Sequence* on pages vi–vii lists the pronunciation points from the twelve units.

V. Follow-Up Activities

In this section, two activities are presented. The teacher may choose to do one or both. The students should be encouraged to incorporate in their discussions the vocabulary and concepts that were presented in the interview or report. It is expected that the students will synthesize the information gathered from the broadcast with their own opinions.

Discussion questions: In groups, the students discuss their answers to one or more of the questions. Students will most likely have different points of view, and should be encouraged to present their views to each other.

Interactive processing activities: Each activity begins with an optional listening and note-taking exercise in which the students listen again to the interview or report for important details. By listening with a particular focus, students will be better prepared to complete the interactive processing activities that follow. The *Scope and Sequence* on pages vi-vii lists the activities from the twelve units. In these activities, students must solve problems or develop ideas that recycle the language and concepts in the interviews and reports. As students complete these activities, they will have an opportunity to examine their beliefs about the issues presented. While each activity has a particular structure, there is ample opportunity for creativity and discussion.

ACKNOWLEDGMENTS

Consider the Issues is dedicated to the memory of Jim Lydon, whose vision and support were instrumental in creating the original text.

The development and realization of the earlier editions of this text would never have been possible without the help, support, and shared ideas of many people. I wish to give special thanks to the following friends and colleagues for providing important insights into the content of this material:

Elaine Cohen, Bernice Cohn, Richard Duffy, John Een, Tess Ferree, Gloria Gallingane, Judy Gilbert, Robert Hertzig, Stephan Hittman, Sherwin Kizner, Bo Knepp, Suma Kurien, Robert Oprandy, Sherry Preiss, Stratten Ray, Joel Rosenfeld, Paul Rudder, Kim Sanabria, Ted Scheffler, Janice Sartori, Peter Thomas, and Linda Tobash.

I also remain grateful to the following staff at National Public Radio for their support and encouragement throughout the earlier process of writing this book:

Wendy Blair, Carolyn Gershfeld, Beth Howard, Frederica Kushner, Carol Iannone, Robert Malesky, Christine Malesky, Margot McGann, Elisabeth Sullivan, and Carol Whitehorn.

I am particularly indebted to Joanne Dresner and Penny Laporte for their vision and guidance in the first editions. Without their continued support I would not have been able to see this text through to its third edition.

Finally, I would like to thank my colleagues—Jane Kenefick, for piloting new material for the third edition of this book, and Linda Lane, for advising me in the development of the pronunciation activities. Special thanks to my husband, Eric Cooper, for sharing his unrelenting positive feedback and support of my work. For this third edition, I would like to thank Mykan White and Andrea Bryant for providing me with invaluable feedback throughout the editing process, and the fabulous Wendy Blair for continuing to execute the production of *Consider the Issues* at National Public Radio!

1

A Courtesy Campaign

A. PREDICTING

From the title, discuss what you think the report in this unit is about.

B. THINKING AHEAD

In groups, discuss your answers to the following questions.

1. Do you own a cell phone? If so, when and where do you typically use it? When and where do you typically *not* use it?

2. Do you think people ever use cell phones inappropriately? If so, give examples.

3. Should cell phone use be controlled in any way? If so, how and in which circumstances?

II. VOCABULARY

Read the following mini-dialogues. The boldfaced words will help you understand the report. Try to determine the meaning of these words from the context. Then circle the letter of the response that makes sense in the dialogue.

1. A: Did you hear that guy's cell phone ringing during the movie?

    B: Yes, that **shrill** sound made me jump out of my seat during the scariest part of the movie.

    A: _____
       a. I know, it did sound rather pretty, didn't it?
       b. Yeah, it sounded like someone was screaming.

2. A: I heard that a suburb in Chicago has **launched a campaign** to make driving with a cell phone illegal. It wants to give out information and get community support for the plan.

    B: _____
       a. So, are people finally beginning to focus on the problem?
       b. I didn't realize there was a law against cell phone use in that area.

3. A: I can't believe how drivers just cut in front of me on the highway.

    B: Yeah, they can be very rude! What's happened to the rules of **etiquette** in this world?

    A: _____
       a. Well, driving laws are different from state to state.
       b. People no longer care about manners, I guess.

4. A: I think cell phone users should try to be more polite when they are using their cell phones in public.

    B: Frankly, I don't **subscribe to** the idea that people can monitor their own behavior. I think they must be forced to change.

    A: _____
       a. So, you must think we need laws to control cell phone use.
       b. So, you must disagree with the proposed laws to control cell phone use.

5. A: I like the policies of that car company!

    B: Why? What makes them so different?

    A: They support good causes. Right now they are **sponsoring** a campaign about using less gas and taking public transportation to work.

B: _____
   a. Doesn't that hurt their business?
   b. Why aren't they in favor of the campaign?

6. A: I hate hearing Dr. Long's cell phone ringing every few minutes.

   B: He should turn the sound off.

   A: Then, how would he know he's getting a call?

   B: Well, he could leave his phone in his pocket and set it on **vibrate**.

   A: _____
      a. But he might not feel it when a call comes in.
      b. No, his answering service isn't very dependable.

7. A: I loved hearing the concert last night!

   B: Yes, so did I. But wasn't that **disruptive** when someone's cell phone rang during the fifth concerto?

   A: _____
      a. Yes, it made me laugh, too.
      b. Yes, it certainly was disturbing.

8. A: I think it's great that more and more communities are making it illegal to drive while talking on cell phones.

   B: It will certainly start to control some of the bad driving I've seen, but I'm afraid of a public **backlash**. People will get mad if they're told they can't drive and talk on the phone.

   A: Why?

   B: _____
      a. I don't know. People get angry when they feel there are too many restrictions.
      b. Well, once driving with cell phones is made illegal, people will want to make everything illegal!

9. A: Oh! There goes another driver on his cell phone. He almost hit someone!

   B: With drivers like that, I don't understand why so many people are opposed to **banning** the use of cell phones while driving.

   A: _____
      a. I guess they've seen too many dangerous incidents with cell phone drivers.
      b. I guess they feel they should have the freedom to use a phone in their cars.

10. A: Why are you so upset?

    B: People are *urging* me to stay another day, but I was excited about going home. I don't know what to do!

    A: _____
       a. Yeah, they should be more supportive of your presence here.
       b. You should stay if they feel it's that important.

11. A: What was the result of the town board meeting last night?

    B: It went well. For one thing, there was a *consensus* that the town should place more restrictions on cell phone use.

    A: _____
       a. What did they argue over?
       b. I'm amazed that people had the same opinion!

III. LISTENING

A. TASK LISTENING

Listen to the report. Find the answer to the following question.

Who is the real Miss Manners? What is her real name?

B. LISTENING FOR MAIN IDEAS

Listen to the report again. The report has been divided into five parts. You will hear a beep at the end of each part. Answer the question for each part in a complete sentence. You should have five statements that make a summary of the report. Compare your summary with that of another student.

Part 1   How is San Diego reacting to cell phone complaints?

_____

_____

Part 2   How did people in San Diego respond to the survey on cell phone use?

_____

_____

Part 3   What reaction have cell phone companies had to San Diego's campaign?

_____

_____

Part 4   According to Judith Martin, why are laws _not_ the best approach to regulating cell phone use?

_____

_____

Part 5   What is the challenge to Mayor Golding's campaign?

_____

_____

C.   LISTENING FOR DETAILS

Read the statements for Part 1. Then listen to Part 1 again and decide whether the statements are true or false. As you listen, write *T* or *F* next to each statement. Compare your answers with those of another student. If you disagree, listen again.

Part 1

_____ 1. More than half of all American adults have wireless telephones.

_____ 2. People are buying wireless telephones at a rate of 46,000 a day.

_____ 3. Most American cities have restricted some use of wireless phones.

_____ 4. There are only a few sacred places left where we aren't disturbed by cell phones.

Repeat the same procedure for Parts 2–5.

Part 2

_____ 5. Reverend Wendy Craig-Purcell is forgiving when cell phones ring during her church service.

_____ 6. San Diego's Mayor Susan Golding conducted a survey on cell phone use on the Internet.

_____ 7. The Mayor responded to the answers to her survey by imposing restrictions on cell phone use in movie theaters.

_____ 8. Part of the courtesy campaign is to display stickers in "quiet zones."

_____ 9. Doug Cohen, a real estate broker, is completely against the use of cell phones.

_____ 10. He believes that cell phone etiquette is similar to driving etiquette.

Part 3

_____ 11. San Diego is the home of many cell phone industries.

_____ 12. Nokia helps support Mayor Golding's courtesy campaign.

_____ 13. The vice president of Nokia thinks that in certain places people should use the vibrate function of cell phones rather than the ringer.

_____ 14. Cell phone companies support the public backlash against cell phones.

_____ 15. Cell phone companies fear government regulation.

_____ 16. Cell phone companies are urging their customers to drink responsibly.

Part 4

_____ 17. According to Judith Martin, the heavy hand of the law is sometimes necessary to control people's cell phone use.

_____ 18. Martin believes people follow different rules when new technologies are introduced.

_____ 19. Martin believes we have about 50% consensus on how to use cell phones.

Part 5

_____ 20. At the news conference, the Mayor's phone vibrates.

_____ 21. She has trouble turning off her phone because she can't find it.

_____ 22. The Nokia vice president shows her how to turn off her phone.

D. LISTENING FOR INFERENCE

Listen to the excerpts from the report. Try to determine the attitude that each speaker has toward people using cell phones in public places. Listen to each speaker's tone of voice and choice of words. Take a few notes as you listen.

Then rank the five speakers according to their tolerance toward annoying cell phone use. Place the number that corresponds to each excerpt in the chart below, with the most tolerant person placed on the left and the least tolerant person placed on the right. Compare your answers with those of another student. Listen to the excerpts again to try and agree on your ranking.

EXCERPT	INTERVIEWEE'S ATTITUDE
Excerpt 1 (Reverend Craig-Purcell)	
Excerpt 2 (Mayor Golding)	
Excerpt 3 (Doug Cohen)	
Excerpt 4 (Larry Paulson)	
Excerpt 5 (Judith Martin)	

Most Tolerant - ➤ Least Tolerant

_____   _____   _____   _____   _____

IV. LOOKING AT LANGUAGE

A. USAGE: Separable Phrasal Verbs

Notice ➤ Listen to the following examples from the report. Notice the grammatical structure of the boldfaced words. Are the structures similar or different? Why?

Examples

1. Vice President Larry Paulson says customers should set their phones to "vibrate" rather than ring in certain settings, and sometimes even ***turn their telephones off***.

2. I think we will influence a lot of people to ***turn off their cell phones*** or to put them on "vibrate."

Explanation

Many verbs in English are composed of two words (verb + preposition). When these two words are combined, they form a phrasal verb and usually have a new meaning. You cannot understand the meaning of these phrasal verbs by just knowing the meaning of the verb and the preposition. They must be learned as a whole.

Some phrasal verbs are separable. In a sentence with a separable two-word verb, the direct object can come between the verb and preposition, or it can come after the verb and preposition.

The phrasal verb *turn off* is an example of a separable phrasal verb. Notice that in the first example, the direct object comes in between the verb and preposition. In the second example, the direct object comes after the verb and preposition; the two parts of the phrasal verb are kept together.

NOTE: If a pronoun is the direct object of the sentence, it *must* come between the verb and preposition; it cannot come after.

Exercise 1

Listen to the following selections from the report. As you listen, underline the phrasal verb in each sentence.

1. And with communities in Ohio and New Jersey already banning cell phone use behind the wheel, the industry may see a courtesy campaign as a way to head off further government regulation. . . .

2. The Mayor later explained that hers was a new phone, and she hadn't figured out all the settings.

3. She got a quick lesson from the Nokia vice president in how to turn off the ringer.

For each previous sentence, find the direct object (if there is one) of the phrasal verb. Rewrite the sentence, placing the direct object between the verb and the preposition.

1. _And with communities in Ohio and New Jersey already banning cell phone use_

   behind the wheel, the industry may see a courtesy campaign as a way to head

   further government regulation off.

2. _____

   _____

3. _____

   _____

Exercise 2

Read the following sentences. Find a phrasal verb below that can replace the underlined word or phrase. Rewrite the sentence using the phrasal verb. Then, find the direct object (if there is one) and move the direct object to separate the phrasal verb.

~~pick up~~	use up	tied up
call up	turn down	give up

1. Most people like the convenience of having a cell phone. They can just <u>take</u> the phone and place a call wherever they are.

   Most people like the convenience of having a cell phone. They can just pick ^the phone^ _up_

   ~~the phone~~ and place a call wherever they are.

2. Although many people complain about others' use of the cell phone, few people are willing to <u>abandon</u> their own cell phone.

   _____

   _____

3. All the emergency calls had <u>clogged</u> the phone lines, so the only way to reach his mother was with a cell phone.

   _____

   _____

4. One way to be more courteous with cell phones is to <u>lower the volume on</u> the ringer in public places.

_____

_____

5. Cell phone companies usually offer some free minutes of calling time each month, but it is easy to <u>consume</u> those free minutes if you like to talk with friends on the phone.

_____

_____

6. One advantage of having a cell phone in your car is that if you're caught in traffic, you can <u>telephone</u> your boss to tell him you are running late.

_____

_____

B.   **PRONUNCIATION: Word Stress in Separable Phrasal Verbs**

Notice ▷   Listen again to the examples from Part A. Which word is stressed, the verb or the preposition? Mark it with a stress mark (').

1. And with communities in Ohio and New Jersey already banning cell phone use behind the wheel, the industry may see a courtesy campaign as a way to ***head off*** further government regulation.

2. The Mayor later explained that hers was a new phone, and she hadn't ***figured out*** all the settings.

3. She got a quick lesson from the Nokia vice president in how to ***turn off*** the ringer.

Explanation   In separable two-word verbs, like in the previous examples, the preposition is stressed. The preposition often receives even more stress when a pronoun comes between the verb and its preposition. If a pronoun replaced the object in the previous sentences, the preposition would be more heavily stressed.

head it **off**   figure them **out**   turn it **off**

Exercise

Work in pairs.   Fill in the blanks in the following dialogues with the correct two-word verb, separated by a pronoun. Then read the dialogues out loud. Be sure to stress the preposition in the two-word verb. Change roles after item 5.

head off	hang up	call off
figure out	call up	use up
~~turn off~~	tie up	throw away

1. A: Jorge's cell phone is so annoying in class!

   B: Yeah. The teacher should just tell him to _____ turn it off _____ before he comes into the classroom.

2. A: I wonder how my parents are doing. I haven't talked to them in ages!

   B: Why don't you just _____ to see how they are?

3. A: My cell phone never works. The ringer doesn't ring, and I can't always make calls when I want to.

   B: If I were you, I would just _____ and get a new one!

4. A: You're always on the phone. You stay on even when I visit you.

   B: OK! Next time I'll _____ as soon as you get here.

5. A: I get 100 free minutes of talk from my cell phone company each month!

   B: Really? I wouldn't know how to _____ since I rarely talk on the phone.

6. A: I can't get through to London. It seems that all the telephone lines are clogged.

    B: I can't imagine what would _____ at this hour!

7. A: Uh oh! My boss gets angry when he sees me using my cell phone at work. Here he comes!

    B: Don't worry. I'll try to _____ at the water fountain to keep him from seeing you.

8. A: This new cell phone is so complicated. I read the instructions, but I can't seem to make it work.

    B: Here. Let me try to _____.

9. A: The meeting was scheduled for 7:30 tomorrow morning, but David and Joy haven't confirmed that they are coming.

    B: Really? Maybe you should _____ and reschedule a meeting for a time when you know everyone will be there.

V. FOLLOW-UP ACTIVITIES

A. DISCUSSION QUESTIONS

In groups, discuss your answers to the following questions.

1. Do you agree that many people have the attitude that "others shouldn't annoy them with their phones" but that "they don't necessarily apply the same rule to themselves"? Do people believe they are in "an etiquette-free zone" while using cell phones? Where else do you see this attitude?

2. Make a list of rules of etiquette that you think people should follow when using cell phones. List your rules according to specific places where cell phones are often used.

B. SURVEY: Cell Phone Courtesy

 1. *Take Notes to Prepare*

San Diego has initiated an unusual campaign to get people to be more courteous with their use of cell phones. By taking notes on the specific complaints about and proposed solutions to cell phone disruptions, you may be better able to interpret public opinion about this issue.

Listen to the report again. Take notes on San Diego's courtesy campaign. Key phrases and some examples have been provided for you. Use your notes to help you formulate questions for the survey that follows.

Places where cell phones are disturbing

• *Churches, libraries* _____

_____

_____

People's complaints about cell phones

_____

_____

_____

Solutions proposed by San Diego's Mayor Golding

_____

_____

_____

Problems with banning cell phone use

_____

_____

_____

2. Survey

Work in a group of four or five students. Write a questionnaire with five *yes/no* questions that ask people's opinions about cell phone courtesy. Your group will interview a variety of people. Decide where and when you will conduct the survey, how many people you will question, who they will be, and so on.

Conduct your survey. Then tally the *yes* and *no* responses and note any significant comments that people made. The following chart can be used to write your questions, tally responses, and record comments. An example has been provided.

Questions	Yes	No	Comments
Do you think people can control their use of cell phones without legal restrictions?	//	///	People never think that they are the problem.

Oral Report

When your group meets again, summarize the information you gathered in your survey. Prepare an oral report to present to the rest of the class. Be sure to include an introduction to your survey, a summary of the results you've gathered, and a conclusion including your own interpretation of your findings.

Oral Presentation Procedures

1. The first student introduces the group and gives an introduction to the survey that was conducted.

2. The next few students present one or two of the questions that were asked, statistics or general responses that were received, and interesting comments that were made by the people who were interviewed. The comments mentioned should help explain why people answered the way they did.

3. The last student concludes the presentation by summarizing the findings from the survey, interpreting them, and perhaps reacting to the results. (For example, "We were surprised to learn that most people thought…")

Useful Words and Phrases

When you talk about the people who answered your survey, you can call them:

- interviewees
- respondents

When you report the information you gathered, you can begin:

- They agreed that . . .
- They felt that . . .
- They believed that . . .
- They stated that . . .

When you indicate the number of people who responded in a certain way, you can say:

- More than half agreed that . . .
- Over 50 percent of the group stated that . . .
- Less than a third said that . . .

"A Courtesy Campaign" was first broadcast on *Morning Edition*, July 25, 2000. The reporter is Scott Horsley.

2

Give Me My Place to Smoke!

I. ANTICIPATING THE ISSUE

A. PREDICTING

From the title, discuss what you think the interview in this unit is about.

B. THINKING AHEAD

In groups, discuss your answers to the following questions.

1. Is smoking common in your country? Describe a typical smoker there.

2. Is the number of women smokers increasing in your country? Why or why not?

3. Is smoking permitted in most public places in your country? Where is smoking restricted?

II. VOCABULARY

The words in the first column will help you understand the interview. Try to guess their meaning from your knowledge of English, or use a dictionary. In each set, cross out the word that does not have a similar meaning. Then compare your answers with those of another student. Discuss the relationship between the words in each set.

1. **secondhand**	used	~~double~~	old
2. **apolitical**	politically involved	politically detached	politically disinterested
3. **cocktail**	mixed drink	alcoholic beverage	after-dinner drink
4. **blabbing**	gossiping	talking foolishly	lecturing
5. **furtively**	openly	secretively	covertly
6. **cognizant**	conscious	intelligent	aware
7. **take a drag**	puff	pull	inhale
8. **defiance**	relief	resistance	refusal
9. **inflict**	force	impose	soften
10. **patrol**	guard	patron	police
11. **knuckled under**	fought	yielded	submitted

III. LISTENING

A. TASK LISTENING

Listen to the interview. Find the answer to the following question.

Who is more tolerant of nonsmokers' attitudes, Peggy or Michael?

B. **LISTENING FOR MAIN IDEAS**

Listen to the interview again. The interview has been divided into five parts. You will hear a beep at the end of each part. Answer the question for each part in a complete sentence. You should have five statements that make a summary of the interview. Compare your summary with that of another student.

Part 1   What has changed about smoking over the years?

_____

_____

Part 2   How has the behavior of smokers changed in people's homes?

_____

_____

Part 3   How have the smoking habits of smokers changed?

_____

_____

Part 4   In what situations do smokers feel defiant?

_____

_____

Part 5   How do Michael and Peggy react differently toward people's feelings about smoking?

_____

_____

C. LISTENING FOR DETAILS

Read the statements for Part 1. Then listen to Part 1 again and decide whether the statements are true or false. As you listen, write *T* or *F* next to each statement. Compare your answers with those of another student. If you disagree, listen again.

Part 1

_____ 1. Peggy has smoked for over 35 years.

_____ 2. Peggy and Michael feel comfortable smoking in their neighborhood bar in Washington, D.C.

_____ 3. The EPA* report on secondhand smoke** will restrict smoking in public places.

_____ 4. Peggy used to give more thought to her smoking 35 years ago.

_____ 5. Peggy thinks today's attitude toward smoking is similar to other attitudes toward freedom.

Repeat the same procedure for Parts 2–5.

Part 2

_____ 6. Fifteen years ago, people offered you an ashtray when you went to their house.

_____ 7. People used to drink, smoke, and talk at the same time at parties.

_____ 8. Smokers at parties now have to stand at the window or outside the house to smoke.

Part 3

_____ 9. Peggy never lights up a cigarette in someone's office or home.

---

* *EPA*: Environmental Protection Agency—U.S. government agency that leads the nation's environmental science, research, education, and assessment effort

** *secondhand smoke*: smoke, exhaled by a smoker, that is inhaled by another person

_____ 10. Michael now blows his smoke straight into the group of people he's with.

_____ 11. Michael looks like a factory when he smokes.

Part 4

_____ 12. Michael has sometimes felt a desire to inflict his habit on others.

_____ 13. Michael feels defiant when someone doesn't want him to smoke in a place where it is permissible to smoke.

_____ 14. Michael believed that the man behind him was physically uncomfortable with his smoking.

_____ 15. Peggy feels defiant toward anyone who wants to judge her behavior.

Part 5

_____ 16. Michael can understand people who don't want to be around smoke.

_____ 17. Michael lives according to the antismoking rules.

_____ 18. Peggy would only consider going to restaurants that don't allow smoking.

_____ 19. Peggy feels smokers should be given equity.

D. LISTENING FOR INFERENCE

Listen to the excerpts from the interview and answer the following questions.
Compare your answers with those of other students.

Excerpt 1

1. How "political" do you think Peggy finds smoking's lack of popularity to be?

   a. very political

   b. somewhat political

   c. not political

Excerpt 2

2. Does Michael feel uncomfortable if he is told not to smoke in someone's house?

   a. Yes, definitely.

   b. No, not at all.

   c. Probably a little.

Excerpt 3

3. Why does Peggy mention the "fur patrol"?

   a. People who judge smoking judge everything, including people who wear fur coats.

   b. People think only rich people who wear fur coats smoke.

   c. People think you're like an animal if you smoke.

IV. LOOKING AT LANGUAGE

A. USAGE: Present Perfect, Present Perfect Progressive, and Simple Past

Notice   Listen to the following examples from the interview. Notice the grammatical structure of the boldfaced words. Are the structures similar or different? When did these events occur?

Examples

1. My name's Michael, and I***'ve been smoking*** for 15 years.

2. My name is Peggy, and I***'ve been smoking*** for probably 30 to 35 years.

3. I***'ve developed*** a whole body language about smoking in groups and in places where it is permissible to smoke.

4. I***'ve*** never ***felt*** a desire to inflict my habit on anybody else.

Explanation   The verb forms used in these examples are the present perfect progressive (the first two examples) and present perfect (the second two examples). These tenses are used to describe a state, activity, or repeated action that began in the past and continues into the present time. Although the two tenses can often be used interchangeably, the present perfect progressive is often used when the continuation of an action is stressed.

| **Present perfect progressive** | **Present perfect** |
| *have* + *been* + (verb)-*ing* | *have* + past participle |

The following chart compares these two verb forms along with the simple past tense.

TENSE	EXAMPLE	MEANING
Present perfect progressive	"My name's Michael, and I**'ve been smoking** for 15 years." "My name is Peggy, and I**'ve been smoking** for probably 30 to 35 years."	Often used when the continuation of an action is stressed. It shows that an activity or state is unfinished.
Present perfect	"I**'ve developed** a whole body language about smoking in groups and in places where it is permissible to smoke." "I**'ve** never **felt** a desire to inflict my habit on anybody else."	Sometimes, a present perfect action is finished. By using the present perfect tense, the result of the action is emphasized. Describes a state, activity, or repeated action that began in the past and continues into the present time.
Simple past	"You **walked** into someone's house and they would offer you an ashtray." "I **was** outside, on the sidewalk."	Describes a completed action at a specific time.

Exercise

Read the following sentences. Use the context of each sentence to choose the best verb form.

1. In recent years, more and more public places _____ smoking.

   a. restricted   b. have been restricting

2. Thirty-five years ago, Peggy _____ a lot of thought to her smoking.

   a. didn't give   b. hasn't given

3. Fifteen years ago, people _____ you an ashtray when you walked into their house.

   a. offered   b. have been offering

4. When Peggy was asked not to smoke in someone's home, she _____ it awkward.

   a. found   b. has found

5. Smoking has become less and less popular. Many of the people Michael sees at parties these days _____ smoking.

   a. gave up   b. have given up

6. During the interview, Michael _____ the smoking style he uses to respect the rights of people who don't want smoke around them.

   a. demonstrated   b. has been demonstrating

7. During the interview, Peggy _____ people to give her a place to smoke.

   a. asked   b. has been asking

8. Peggy and Michael feel that their acceptance as smokers _____.

   a. has been changing   b. has changed

B. **PRONUNCIATION: Stress Changes with the *a-* Prefix**

Notice

Listen to the following example from the interview. Focus on the boldfaced word. Which syllable is stressed in this word?

And I don't know how much of that is basically political and how much is ***apolitical.***

Explanation

The prefix *a-* is used in two ways. As a negative prefix, it means "not" or "without." When it is added to a base word, the stress is placed on the prefix and the pronunciation is /ey/. Notice the stress change from *political* to *apolitical* in the example above.

The prefix *a-* can also have a different (not negative) meaning. It can mean "in a particular condition or way." In this case, the prefix is *not* stressed and *a-* is pronounced /ə/, such as in the words *arise* and *abreast.*

When other negative prefixes, such as *un-*, *dis-*, and so on are added to base words, the stress pattern does not usually change:

'common	un'common
re'spectful	dis'respectful
under'stood	misunder'stood
'logical	il'logical
'regular	ir'regular

Exercise

Work in pairs.

Student A: Read the questions or statements in the left-hand column to Student B. Check Student B's responses for the correct stress and pronunciation of the words with *a-* prefixes.

Student B: Cover the left-hand column. Respond to Student A using one of the vocabulary words in the box. Be sure to consider the stress and pronunciation of the words with *a-* prefixes. Switch roles after item 5.

aboard	asymmetrical
alike	atheist
amass	

Student A

1. I'd sure like to go on the boat ride with you! (Student B: a'board)

2. What is it that's strange about his face? (Student B: 'asymmetrical)

3. Why don't you ever go to church? (Student B: 'atheist)

4. George and Mara have so many similar interests. (Student B: a'like)

5. How did your grandparents become so rich? (Student B: a'mass)

Student B

1. Well, come along. Just climb _____!

2. Well it's a bit _____, but I find him handsome!

3. You know, I'm not an _____. I just don't like that church.

4. Yes, they've been together so long that they are very much _____.

5. They spent their lifetime working hard and were able to _____ millions of dollars!

Now change roles. A becomes B and B becomes A.

ablaze	atypical
amoral	awaken
anew	

Student B

6. I heard there was a huge fire in the city last night. (Student A: a'blaze)

7. Why can't you and your co-workers get along? (Student A: a'new)

8. I really think that guy deserves to go to jail! (Student A: 'amoral)

9. What's wrong with your boss? He seems a little strange. (Student A: 'atypical)

10. I'm so tired that I think I could sleep for days! (Student A: a'waken)

Student A

6. Yes, the whole downtown area was _____, but most people were saved.

7. I know we've had problems, but yesterday we decided we would start _____.

8. I agree. Not only did he commit a robbery, but his behavior is so _____.

9. He is rather _____, but he's quite creative, and he's a fun person to work for!

10. I'll tell the children not to _____ you in the morning so that you can get a good night's sleep.

V. FOLLOW-UP ACTIVITIES

A. DISCUSSION QUESTIONS

In groups, discuss your answers to the following questions.

1. Should cigarette smoking be permitted in public places? If so, in which places?

2. Do you think smoking will eventually be made illegal? Are the smoking restrictions in the United States a sign of what will happen in other countries, or are Americans unique in their current reaction to smoking?

3. Do you think tobacco should be classified as a drug?

B.   DEBATE: Smoking in Public Places

1. Take Notes to Prepare

By focusing on the interview's comparisons of attitudes toward smoking years ago and today, you will be better able to conduct a debate in the exercise that follows.

Listen to the interview again. Take notes on how attitudes toward smoking have changed over the years. Key phrases and some examples have been provided for you. Use your notes in the debate that follows to help you discuss the pros and cons of smoking in public places.

	Years ago	**Today**
Smokers' attitudes toward their smoking	• didn't give a lot of thought to it	• keenly aware of others' perceptions
		• realize it's much less popular
Smoking at people's homes		
Smoking at parties		

Smokers' habits

   _____   _____

   _____   _____

   _____   _____

   _____   _____

   _____   _____

2. Debate

Divide into two teams to debate smoking in public places.

Team A will argue in favor of smoking in public places.

> You believe that smokers have the right to smoke in public places. You will argue in favor of providing smoking sections in restaurants, theaters, on public transportation, and so on, so that smokers can have the opportunity to smoke if they wish.

Team B will argue in favor of prohibiting smoking in public places.

> You believe that smokers should not have the right to smoke in public places. You will argue in favor of prohibiting smoking in theaters, on public transportation, and so on, because you feel it is unpleasant and unhealthy* for nonsmokers even when people smoke in designated areas.

Prepare your arguments. Choose a moderator to lead the debate. The moderator will time the presentations and keep order during the debate.

Debate Procedures

1. Each team meets separately to prepare a list of arguments. (You may want to plan which team member will present which argument during the debate.)

2. During the preparation, each team tries to predict arguments that the other team will make; then it finds arguments against each of these.

3. Team A and Team B sit facing each other. The moderator sits off to the side, in the middle. (You may want to set a time limit for the whole debate.)

---

* Reports have shown that secondhand smoke is unhealthy for nonsmokers.

4. The moderator begins the debate by asking one of the teams to introduce the issue and present the first argument in one minute or less.

5. A member of the opposing team responds in one minute or less. This back-and-forth format continues. After a member of one team has spoken, only a member of the opposing team may respond. Two members of the same team may not make arguments one after the other.

6. The moderator announces when there are two minutes remaining, giving each team one final chance to make an argument.

7. At the end of the debate, the moderator evaluates the strength of each team's arguments.

"Give Me My Place to Smoke!" was first broadcast on *All Things Considered*, **January 9, 1993. The interviewer is Katie Davis.**

3

Kids and the Media

Student witnesses of a school shooting in Germany being questioned by journalists

I. ANTICIPATING THE ISSUE

A. PREDICTING

From the title, discuss what you think the report in this unit is about.

B. THINKING AHEAD

In groups, discuss your answers to the following questions.

1. Do you think children should be interviewed by the media in breaking news events?

2. What are the advantages and disadvantages of interviewing kids in major news stories?

II. VOCABULARY

Read the text. The boldfaced words will help you understand the report. Try to determine the meaning of these words. Write the number of each word next to its definition or synonym in the list at the end of the text.

With events being broadcast every minute internationally, journalists have taken on an important role in the world. With this important role, they have come under **scrutiny** by the public. People have become very critical of journalists and their need to **scoop** the competition. Journalists will sometimes do anything to be the first to print an important news story; they will look for any way to get to the source of that story. But what happens when that source is a child? How does a journalist **ascertain** whether or not it is appropriate to interview a child during a tragic event? If a journalist does present a story from a child's perspective, how should he or she **couch** it in the report to make it more acceptable? Interviewing children during a crisis is perhaps one of the most controversial **ethical** issues in journalism today.

One of the reasons it may not be a good idea to interview children is because of their **vulnerability**. Children are usually too young to understand the **trauma** they are involved in, and asking them to report on tragic events could be hurtful. This issue was best illustrated during the well-known Elian Gonzalez case, in which a six-year-old boy was found floating in the sea off the coast of Florida, after his boat, which he and 13 others had used to escape from Cuba, had sunk. His mother, one of the 13, had died in the boat accident. Elian was turned over to his great uncle in Florida. Elian's father, in Cuba, demanded his son's return. For months, the families fought over where Elian would live. This argument led to a political battle, which lasted for months, between the United States and Cuba. Journalists gave important coverage to the story, **grilling** members of the family for information on a daily basis. Some even went as far as interviewing Elian about the loss of his mother and whether he thought he should live in the United States or in Cuba. But such questions are generally **beyond the grasp**[9] of a six-year-old. Critics felt that, by asking him difficult questions and bringing up sensitive subjects, journalists had a negative effect on Elian's feelings of security.

In addition to children's vulnerability when interviewed by the media, moral issues are also raised because journalists may be putting children's lives in danger by interviewing them "live on the scene." This problem was illustrated during the Columbine High School massacre in the United States, when two students, Eric Harris and Dylan Klebold, entered their school with weapons and killed 13 people, including themselves. The **perpetrators**[10] had also injured 25 others. During the tragic event, some students in and around the school were able to call out on their cell phones. Some even spoke to the media. But critics said that these cell-phone calls with journalists could have helped Harris and Klebold **pinpoint**[11] victims they could not have found otherwise. The interviews with kids in the school during the shootings could have provided information about where kids were hiding. In other words, getting the story as it was happening may not have been in the best interest of the students in the school.

It is not clear what role children should play in reporting events to the media. In fact, there seem to be no **bedrock rules**[12] concerning children and the media. In a crisis situation, there may be no time for **parental consent**[13]. Children are sometimes essential for reporting events, especially when they are the only witnesses. But as the media continues to play a key role in how the public understands world events, the role of children and the media must be considered when discussing ethics in journalism.

_____ a. express something in a particular way in order not to offend someone

_____ b. beat, perform better than

_____ c. a very bad and upsetting experience

_____ d. asking someone a lot of difficult questions

_____ e. find out

_____ f. find the exact position of something or someone

_____ g. basic ideas and principles

_____ h. state of being easily harmed or hurt emotionally, physically, or morally

__1__ i. careful examination of someone or something

_____ j. too difficult for

_____ k. criminals

_____ l. permission by parents for their child to do something

_____ m. relating to principles of what is right and wrong

III. ▶ LISTENING

A. TASK LISTENING

Listen to the report. Find the answer to the following question.

Who provided the tape of Elian Gonzalez that aired on the evening news?

B. LISTENING FOR MAIN IDEAS

Listen to the report again. The report has been divided into four parts. You will hear a beep at the end of each part. Choose the best answer for each question. Compare your answers with those of another student. Try to agree on the answers.

Part 1   What is the subject of this report?

a. who the children are in the news

b. how the media uses children as sources for the news

Part 2   What issue in journalism was raised in the reporting of the Elian Gonzalez case?

    a.   interviewing people from different countries during a crisis

    b.   interviewing very young children in a crisis

Part 3   According to Bob Steel, what should journalists think about?

    a.   the maturity of the child interviewed

    b.   the age of the child interviewed

Part 4   What issue in journalism was raised in the reporting of the Columbine High School shootings?

    a.   whether or not journalists should cover children during a crisis

    b.   whether or not journalists should use cell phones for interviews

C.   LISTENING FOR DETAILS

Read the statements for Part 1. Listen to Part 1 of the report again and fill in the blanks with the missing information. Do the same for Parts 2–4. Compare your answers with those of another student.

Part 1

1.   The media has been under scrutiny over how _____ are used as sources in news stories.

2.   _____ was criticized for airing an interview with Elian Gonzalez.

3.   _____ was criticized for broadcasting phone calls made during the Columbine High School shootings.

Part 2

4. Diane Sawyer referred to one of the bedrock rules of the craft of journalism:

   "Get the story _____."

5. According to Sawyer, one of the things that none of the journalists had done was

   _____ .

6. Bob Steel objected to journalists asking Elian questions about

   _____ or staying in the United States, or

   _____ because they were beyond the grasp of the six-year old.

Part 3

7. An immature child might mix up _____ and

   _____ in answering questions.

8. Maturity becomes even more of a pressing concern when

   _____ or criminal allegations are at stake.

9. Steel says journalists need to _____ enough to assess the

   situation and ascertain _____ a witness may have.

Part 4

10. Witnesses to a crime may be vulnerable if _____ goes after

    them.

11. In theory, the perpetrators in Columbine High School could have used

    _____ to pinpoint their intended victims.

12. Suzanne McCarroll's ability to judge _____ is a matter of

    gut instinct.*

    *gut instinct: reaction or feeling that you are sure is right although you cannot give a reason for it

13. When interviewing kids, parental consent doesn't mean much because parents are sometimes _____, and they sometimes give consent for the wrong reason.

14. McCarroll says that when kids are concerned, the bottom line is

_____.

15. The question Bob Steel thinks listeners, readers, and viewers need to keep in mind when watching the evening news is: "_____?"

D. LISTENING FOR INFERENCE

Listen to the excerpts from the report. Do you think it is likely or unlikely that the statements reflect the attitude of the speaker? Circle the number on the voting scales below that corresponds to your interpretation. Discuss your ratings with other students to see if you agree.

Excerpt 1 (Diane Sawyer)

1. The media has misrepresented Elian Gonzalez.

Likely				Unlikely
1	2	3	4	5

2. Too many stories have been written about Elian.

Likely				Unlikely
1	2	3	4	5

Excerpt 2 (Bob Steel)

3. Diane Sawyer is not a good journalist.

Likely				Unlikely
1	2	3	4	5

4. Journalists should not interview six-year-olds.

Likely				Unlikely
1	2	3	4	5

Excerpt 3 (Suzanne McCarroll)

5. McCarroll wouldn't have interviewed Elian Gonzalez.

Likely				**Unlikely**
1	2	3	4	5

6. McCarroll is glad she's not in the position of a leading TV reporter like Diane Sawyer in the Elian Gonzalez case.

Likely				**Unlikely**
1	2	3	4	5

IV.   LOOKING AT LANGUAGE

A.   USAGE: Modal Perfects

Notice   Listen to the following example from the report. Discuss the verb form of the boldfaced words. What is the meaning?

> CNN and a local Denver television station were criticized last year when they broadcast this tape and others like it: cell-phone calls from students hiding in and around Columbine High School, which Dylan Klebold and Eric Harris **could**, in theory, **have used** to pinpoint the locations of their intended victims.

Explanation   In the above example, a modal perfect form of the verb is used to make a statement about the past. In this statement, the reporter refers to a possible action in the past that was not taken.

Below, the different forms of modal perfects are used in the same sentence. Notice the differences in meaning. Each modal perfect is presented in both the active (A) and passive (P) voice.

MODAL PERFECT	EXAMPLE	MEANING
Might have	(A) The reporters **might have interviewed** Elian. (P) Elian **might have been interviewed.**	The writer is not sure whether or not Elian was interviewed. He is making a logical deduction but is only 50% sure.
Could have	(A) The reporters **could have interviewed** Elian. (P) Elian **could have been interviewed.**	The writer refers to possible action in the past that was not taken. Interviewing Elian was a possibility but the reporters, chose not to do it. OR As with *might have,* the writer is not sure whether or not the reporters interviewed Elian.
Must have	(A) The reporters **must have interviewed** Elian. (P) Elian **must have been interviewed.**	The writer is quite certain (90%) that the action did happen. The writer was not at the scene, but judging from other observations or information, he can deduce that the reporters did interview Elian.
Should have	(A) The reporters **should have interviewed** Elian. (P) Elian **should have been interviewed.**	Elian was not interviewed. The writer is providing advice or an opinion contrary to what actually happened.

Exercise

Complete the following statements with the verb in parentheses and the correct
modal perfect. Use the information from Rick Karr's report as the context for sentence
meaning. Use negative forms when necessary. Consider active and passive voice.

1. People who criticized CNN for using Elian as a news source (think)

   ___*must have thought*___ he was too young to be interviewed.

2. Bob Steel thinks that Elian Gonzalez (interview) _____

   about the loss of his mother.

3. Elian Gonzalez (know) _____ fact from fantasy when he

   was interviewed.

4. Only a mature adult (comment) _____ effectively on

   international relations or criminal allegations involved in the Elian Gonzalez case.

5. Some feel that a tape of cell-phone calls within Columbine High School

   (broadcast) _____ by CNN and a local Denver television

   station.

6. Suzanne McCarroll (use) _____ good judgment in

   interviewing kids at Columbine since she won the praise of media critics.

7. McCarroll (have) _____ a clear idea of whether or not she

   would have interviewed Elian Gonzalez since she hesitated so much when asked.

8. The family-made tape of Elian Gonzalez (present) _____

   with more sensitivity by the media.

B. PRONUNCIATION: Reductions of *Have*

Notice Listen to the following example from the report. Focus on the boldfaced verb. What is the meaning?

REPORTER: So . . . had she been in Diane Sawyer's shoes, would she have interviewed Elian?

MCCARROLL: I don't know . . . I . . . you know, I would hate to . . . , I don't know. I . . . truthfully, I guess I don't think I **would've**. But I'm not in her position.

Explanation In spoken English, *have* is reduced when it is not the main verb. When reduced, *have* is pronounced [əv], like the preposition *of*. In the example above, McCarroll is saying "I don't think I would **have** interviewed Elian."

Exercise

Work in pairs.

Student A: Read the questions or statements in the left-hand column to Student B. Check Student B's responses with the correct response in parentheses. Listen for the reduced form of *have* in Student B's responses.

Student B: Cover the left-hand column. Respond to Student A using a short-answer with *would've*, *might've*, *must've*, *could've*, or *should've*. Switch roles after item 5.

Student A

1. Did Diane Sawyer think her interview

   with Elian Gonzalez was special?

   (Student B: must've)

2. Did you hear that Diane Sawyer asked

   Elian Gonzalez about the loss of his mother?

   (Student B: should've)

3. Do you think the six-year-old boy knew

   fact from fantasy? (Student B: could've)

Student B

1. I'm not sure, but she _____.

2. I know, and I don't think she

   _____.

3. No, I don't think he

   _____.

4. The journalists didn't fight the urge to get the story "right this second." (Student B: should've)

4. I know, but they _____.

5. If Diane Sawyer had covered the Columbine High School shootings, do you think she would have interviewed kids on the scene? (Student B: would've)

5. Hmm . . . I think she probably _____.

Now change roles. A becomes B and B becomes A.

Student B

6. Did cell-phone calls within Columbine High School help Klebold and Harris pinpoint more victims? (Student A: could've)

Student A

6. No, but I'm sure they _____.

7. Did Suzanne McCarroll win praise for her handling of Columbine because she was sensitive toward the kids she interviewed? (Student A: must've)

7. Yes, I think she _____.

8. Did the television reporters present the home-made video of Elian Gonzalez with sensitivity? (Student A: should've)

8. Apparently not, but they _____.

9. Do you think the media hurt Elian with all the attention? (Student A: might've/could've)

9. It's hard to say, but they _____.

10. If Suzanne McCarroll had covered the Elian Gonzalez story, would she have interviewed him? (Student A: would've)

10. No, she didn't think she _____.

V. FOLLOW-UP ACTIVITIES

A. DISCUSSION QUESTIONS

In groups, discuss your answers to the following questions.

1. Do you think young people can help tell the story in a big media event? Can a child know fact from fantasy?

2. Do you agree with the following statement made by the reporter Rick Karr?

    > Journalism is a deeply competitive field, and sometimes the urge to scoop the competition trumps the gut check.

    This statement means that journalists may sometimes be tempted to do unethical reporting in order to be the first to report a story. Do you agree that this is a problem in the field of journalism? Can you think of other examples where competition gets in the way of rational decision making?

B. DEBATE: Interviewing Children in the Media

1. Take Notes to Prepare

By focusing on the problem of reporters interviewing kids in crisis situations, you will be better able to conduct a debate in the exercise that follows.

Listen to the report again. Take notes on the problems of interviewing kids in the media. Key phrases and some examples have been provided for you. Then, work with another student and think of reasons why the media might want to interview kids. Some of the points are suggested in the report. Use your notes in the debate that follows to help you discuss the pros and cons of interviewing children in the media.

	Problems with Interviewing Kids	Reasons for Interviewing Kids
Getting information from the source	Kids not mature enough.	They may speak the truth!
Kids as witnesses		
Presentation of news		

2. Debate

Divide into two teams to debate the appropriateness of children being interviewed by the media.

Team A will argue in favor of the media's interviewing children.

> You believe that the media have the right to interview anybody who will help them report a story accurately. You will argue in favor of complete access to everybody, including children.

Team B will argue against the media's interviewing children.

> You believe that there should be some limitations regarding who the media can interview. Children, in particular, may not be too upset or nervous to talk to the media, and the information they give may not be correct.

Prepare your arguments. Choose a moderator to lead the debate. The moderator will time the presentations and keep order during the debate.

Debate Procedures

1. Each team meets separately to prepare a list of arguments. (You may want to plan which team member will present which argument during the debate.)

2. During the preparation, each team tries to predict arguments that the other team will make; then it finds arguments against each of these.

3. Team A and Team B sit facing each other. The moderator sits off to the side, in the middle. (You may want to set a time limit for the whole debate.)

4. The moderator begins the debate by asking one of the teams to introduce the issue and present the first argument in one minute or less.

5. A member of the opposing team responds in one minute or less. This back-and-forth format continues. After a member of one team has spoken, only a member of the opposing team may respond. Two members of the same team may not make arguments one after the other.

6. The moderator announces when there are two minutes remaining, giving each team one final chance to make an argument.

7. At the end of the debate, the moderator evaluates the strength of each team's arguments.

"Kids and the Media" was first broadcast on *Weekend All Things Considered*, April 16, 2000. The reporter is Rick Karr.

4

Is It a Sculpture, or Is It Food?

I. ANTICIPATING THE ISSUE

A. PREDICTING

From the title, discuss what you think the interview in this unit is about.

B. THINKING AHEAD

In groups, discuss your answers to the following questions.

1. What do you know about genetic engineering? In what areas of life is it being used today?

2. When you buy fruits and vegetables, which is more important to you: taste, texture, color, nutritional value, price, or how long something stays fresh? Why?

3. Have you ever eaten food that was genetically engineered? How did you know it was genetically engineered? What did it look like? What did it taste like?

II. ▶ VOCABULARY

Read the text. The boldfaced words will help you understand the interview. Try to determine the meaning of these words. Write the number of each word next to its definition or synonym in the list at the end of the text.

Experiments in genetic engineering have created important **breakthroughs**[1] in many areas; they have led to cures for many diseases, the control of insect populations, and the improvement of food production. However, most of these experiments are not **foolproof**[2]; no one knows for sure what negative consequences they could have.

People often **poke fun at**[3] progress, possibly because technology often presents new problems as it attempts to solve old ones. Imagine what might happen to genes that have been genetically engineered in scientists' laboratories once they are released into the environment. The **ramifications**[4] of introducing these genes could be terrifying. Some people have a name for genetically manipulated food: "Frankenfood."

Whether or not the fear of science-fiction food is realistic, genetically engineered food has received a great deal of attention recently because many of these food products are now on the market. For example, gene-spliced fruits and vegetables have been developed to improve their color, taste, and shelf life. Some people are concerned that these foods don't have the same taste as natural foods, or that they may cause people to become sick. For example, trout genes are now used to produce longer-lasting tomatoes. Yet, people who have **allergies**[5] to fish may become ill eating these tomatoes if the trout gene has not been sufficiently **sublimated**[6] in the gene-splicing process. Restaurant owners, as well as others who work with food, have started to **boycott**[7] these foods to show their disagreement with this type of food production.

On the other hand, many people recognize that genetically manipulated food can bring many benefits to our lives. It could increase food production throughout the world and begin to solve the hunger problem. It could improve the taste and shelf life of food. Genetically engineered food could also ***alleviate*** our dependence on pesticides to protect crops; if fewer pesticides were used, the problem of pesticide ***residue*** in food could be reduced. Finally, these foods could be a ***boon*** to the food industry, which could help the ***fragile*** world economy.

Most people will agree that more information is needed before we can be sure that genetically engineered food will improve our lives. We need to weigh the advantages with the disadvantages, as well as consider the dangers, before we make further commitments to experimenting in this area.

_____ a. something that is useful and makes your life easier

_____ b. condition that makes you sick from certain things

_____ c. weakened

_____ d. easily damaged or ruined

_____ e. make something less bad or severe

_____ f. results that have effects on other things

_____ g. certain to be successful; always effective

_____ h. new discoveries

_____ i. something remaining; part of something that is left after something else disappears

_____ j. refuse to use or buy as a way of protesting

_____ k. joke about; make fun of

III. LISTENING

A. TASK LISTENING

Listen to the interview. Find the answer to the following question.

Is Joyce Goldstein more in favor of or more against genetically engineered food?

B. LISTENING FOR MAIN IDEAS

Listen to the interview again. The interview has been divided into four parts. You will hear a beep at the end of each part. A word or phrase has been given to help you focus on the main idea of each part. Write the main idea in a complete sentence. You should have four statements that make a summary of the interview. Compare your summary with that of another student.

Part 1   boycott

Chefs from around the country have boycotted genetically engineered food.

_____

Part 2   the tomato

_____

_____

Part 3   lack of information

_____

_____

Part 4   right to know

_____

_____

C. LISTENING FOR DETAILS

Read the statements for Part 1. Then listen to Part 1 again and decide whether the statements are true or false. As you listen, write *T* or *F* next to each statement. Compare your answers with those of another student. If you disagree, listen again.

Part 1

_____ 1. Genetically designed tomatoes are now* available in the supermarket.

_____ 2. Genetically engineered cheese can now* be purchased.

_____ 3. World hunger may be helped with genetically engineered food.

_____ 4. Over 1,000 chefs decided not to serve genetically engineered food.

_____ 5. Special labeling is required for genetically engineered food.

Repeat the same procedure for Parts 2–4.

Part 2

Goldstein believes . . .

_____ 6. the genetically engineered tomato is being produced for flavor.

_____ 7. the use of fish genes in tomatoes is a good idea.

_____ 8. these foods should be thoroughly tested and labeled before they are sold.

Part 3

According to Goldstein . . .

_____ 9. the methods of the old days were better than those today.

_____ 10. genetically bred roses are very beautiful and smell good.

_____ 11. restaurants shouldn't serve genetically engineered food until it is tested.

* at the time the interview was recorded

_____ 12. we should worry about corporate profit.

_____ 13. the Food and Drug Administration* does a good job of regulating these foods.

Part 4

According to Goldstein . . .

_____ 14. pesticide residue in foods is a problem.

_____ 15. genetic manipulation of foods to reduce their dependence on pesticides is a good thing.

_____ 16. the crossing of trout with tomatoes is a good thing.

_____ 17. genetic experimentation should help improve the taste of food.

_____ 18. what is good for agribusiness is generally good for the consumer.

_____ 19. consumers are given the information they need in purchasing food.

D. LISTENING FOR INFERENCE

Listen to the excerpts from the interview and answer the following questions. Compare your answers with those of other students.

Excerpt 1

1. How does Goldstein feel about "progress?" Why does she put it in quotes?

_____

_____

Excerpt 2

2. What is Goldstein's view of the Food and Drug Administration?

_____

_____

* _Food and Drug Administration:_ U.S. government organization that regulates the sale and use of food and drugs

Excerpt 3

3. How sure is Goldstein that agribusiness will work toward making foods that are good for the consumer?

_____

_____

IV. ▶ LOOKING AT LANGUAGE

A. USAGE: Restrictive Adjective Clauses

Notice ▷ Listen to the following example from the interview. Discuss the function of the boldfaced words. What part of speech could replace the group of boldfaced words (noun, verb, adjective, adverb)?

In the near future, you might be able to buy a tomato in the supermarket *that has been genetically designed and engineered. . . .*

Explanation ▷ The boldfaced words above are an example of an adjective clause. Adjective clauses can make language more sophisticated in both writing and speaking. Rather than expressing an idea in two simple sentences that repeat the same noun, you can replace the noun in one sentence with a relative pronoun (*who, which, that*). This changes two simple sentences into one more complex sentence.

In the near future, you might be able to buy a tomato in the supermarket.	The tomato has been genetically designed and engineered.
<ul><li>delete period from first sentence</li><li>replace "the tomato" from second sentence with relative pronoun "that"</li><li>combine sentences</li></ul>	
In the near future, you might be able to buy a tomato in the supermarket that has been genetically designed and engineered.	

Exercise

Listen to the following selection from the interview. Underline the adjective clauses.
Circle the relative pronouns, and draw arrows to the nouns they describe.

In the near future, you might be able to buy a tomato in the supermarket (that) has

been genetically designed and engineered, a tomato that would stay ripe much

longer, strawberries that are not so fragile in freezing temperatures, vegetable oil

that's lower in fat. Already on the market: a gene-spliced product that's used in

cheese making. There are impressive claims being made for genetic manipulation

of food, including production increases that could help alleviate world hunger.

But there's also concern, and indeed some fear, about the use of gene-splicing

techniques. . . .

B. PRONUNCIATION: Listing Intonation

Notice

Listen to the following example from the interview. Focus on the list of
foods that may be sold in the future. Determine whether each underlined
phrase has a rising or falling intonation pattern. Draw a rising (⌣➚) or
falling (⎯➘) arrow over each underlined phrase to show the intonation
pattern. Are the patterns similar or different? Why?

In the near future, you may be able to buy a tomato in the supermarket that has

been genetically designed and engineered, a tomato that would stay ripe much

longer, strawberries that are not so fragile in freezing temperatures, vegetable

oil that's lower in fat.

Explanation

When speakers list items, they tend to use a rising intonation for each item
until they finish. As in the example above, this rising intonation indicates to
the listener that the speaker could go on, or that there may be more
examples that the speaker cannot think of. The list is unfinished.

The items of the list can be phrases, like those in the previous example, or they can be single words. Each item is pronounced together as a thought group.

If the list is finished, however, the last item has a rise-fall pattern. Generally, the conjunction *and* or *or* introduces the final item of the list. Listen for the rising intonation of the first three items in the following statement. The fourth item, which is the last item, has a rise-fall pattern to indicate that the speaker has finished.

The genetically-engineered foods that are mentioned in the interview are tomatoes, strawberries, oil, and cheese.

Exercise

Read the following mini-dialogues. Draw the intonation patterns for each underlined item in the lists.

Work in pairs. Practice reading the dialogues with the correct intonation patterns. Switch roles after item 3.

1. A: Which foods are being genetically designed these days?

    B: Primarily fruits and vegetables such as tomatoes, strawberries, melons . . .

2. A: Why are foods being genetically engineered?

    B: To resist freezing temperatures, stay ripe much longer, and maintain a
    longer shelf life!

3. A: Why is Joyce Goldstein concerned about genetically altered food?

    B: She is worried about fish allergies, pesticide residue, and corporate profit.

4. A: What is the effect of genetically engineering food?

    B: The food is changed in terms of its look, taste, smell . . .

5. A: Which groups are expressing their views about genetically engineered food?

B: Lots of people are voicing their opinions: <u>restaurant chefs</u>, <u>agribusiness</u>,

<u>the Food and Drug Administration</u> . . .

6. A: What good points does Goldstein mention about genetically altered roses?

B: She says that they're <u>beautiful to look at</u>, <u>good to smell</u>, and <u>bred safely</u>.

V. FOLLOW-UP ACTIVITIES

A. DISCUSSION QUESTIONS

In groups, discuss your answers to the following questions.

1. Should genetically engineered food be boycotted by restaurant owners, supermarket owners, consumers in general?

2. Should the government require special labeling for genetically engineered foods? If so, what information should be on the label?

3. Some people have called genetically engineered food "science-fiction food" or even "Frankenfood." Do you think human beings' manipulation of nature benefits or harms society? Can you think of other examples of how human beings manipulate nature? How do you feel about it?

B. VALUES CLARIFICATION: Genetic Experimentation

1. Take Notes to Prepare

By focusing on Joyce Goldstein's concerns about genetically engineered food, you may be better able to see the pros and cons of genetic engineering in other areas as well.

Listen to the interview again. Take notes on the benefits and disadvantages of genetic engineering. Key phrases and some examples have been provided for you. Use your notes to help you in the values clarification exercise that follows.

Benefits of genetic engineering

• _longer-life tomatoes_ _____

_____

_____

_____

_____

_____

_____

Disadvantages of genetic engineering

• _gene-splicing techniques not clear_ _____

_____

_____

_____

_____

_____

_____

✔ 2. **Values Clarification**

Work in groups. Read the following proposals for experiments involving genetic engineering. Note the public's concern about the danger of each experiment.

Decide which of these experiments should be conducted. Rank these choices from the one you think is the most important (1) to the one you think is the least important (5) for improving today's world. Try to reach a group consensus.

_____ Character Trait Selection

These experiments would attempt to transfer genes to embryos and develop the cloning process. By selecting and transferring special genes to animals, scientists and farmers could create larger and stronger livestock. These experiments could lead to a system for human gene selection. Parents would be able to choose the genetic traits of their children.

Public concern: Choosing character traits for people is not ethical. In addition, it is cruel to animals to use them for this kind of experimentation.

_____ Cure for Diseases

These experiments would develop a cure for diseases by manipulating genes in humans. Scientists hope to clone genes in order to treat patients and eventually develop a cure for diseases.

Public concern: The treatment could affect normal cells in the body and hurt the patient. Side effects from these drugs might be passed on to future generations.

_____ Increase World Food Supply

These experiments would field-test genetically engineered bacteria on crops to help control damage from cold weather. Experimental pesticides would also be developed through genetic engineering to use in farming. These experiments would also improve the shelf life of fruits and vegetables. More food could be produced for developing countries.

Public concern: The experimentation may cause gene mutation that could be irreversible. No one is really sure what effect this field testing would have on the environment. Introducing new organisms into the earth's environment could be damaging. The splicing of food genes could result in allergies that people are unaware of.

_____ **Military Development**

These experiments would attempt to create biological weapons by means of gene splicing and recombining DNA.* Some countries are already working on these experiments and could become very powerful with these new weapons.

Public concern: The development of these weapons could increase the possibilities of biological warfare.

_____ **Fertility Regulation**

These experiments would attempt to clone hormones to regulate fertility in humans. Experiments would also develop techniques for artificial insemination and embryo transfer.

Public concern: The hormones could get out of control and a person might become "too fertile," conceiving more children than desired. Fertilization experiments tamper with nature.

* *DNA*: Deoxyribonucleic acid—acid located in the nucleus of a cell that carries genetic information

"Is It a Sculpture, or Is It Food?" was first broadcast on *All Things Considered*, August 3, 1992. The interviewer is Noah Adams.

5

What's Happening to Home?

A. PREDICTING

From the title, discuss what you think the interview in this unit is about.

B. THINKING AHEAD

In groups, discuss your answers to the following questions.

1. What is the meaning of "home" to you? What feelings do you get when you think of home?

2. How has technology changed the worlds of work and home? Give examples. Are the changes more positive or more negative, in your opinion?

II. VOCABULARY

Read the sentences in the box. Then read the numbered sentences that follow the box. After each numbered sentence, write the sentence from the box that most logically follows, based on the meaning of the boldfaced word.

In that **refuge**, they were protected.

Every day more cultures mix in this type of **fusion**.

It's a **phenomenon** that's sure to be seen more and more over time.

It's unclear and a bit of a **blur**.

That was a **eureka** moment that changed my life.

The water was **seeping** into our tent from the wet ground beneath.

The faucet had been **leaking** for days.

Look, it's **bleeding** through and making a mark on the table.

We need to set some sort of **boundary** to limit his visits.

This little piece of technology is the world's favorite **gadget**!

She always finds herself in **dilemmas**.

---

1. I'll never forget when I finally learned how to drive a car.

   That was a eureka moment that changed my life.

2. When I got home from vacation there was a flood in my bathroom!

   _____

3. With immigration have come new combinations of ethnic foods and international music.

   _____

4. I can't see where the sky begins and where the horizon ends in this painting.

   _____

5. These days everybody seems to have a cell phone!

_____

6. Mara can't decide whether to go back to work or quit her job and stay home with the children.

_____

7. Josh stops by to see us almost every night just when we're sitting down to dinner!

_____

8. The climbers moved down the mountain to a small cave before the dangerous storm arrived.

_____

9. You shouldn't have put the tomato in that paper napkin.

_____

10. These days, more and more people are staying home to work.

_____

11. It never stopped raining the whole night.

_____

III. ▶ LISTENING

A. TASK LISTENING

Listen to the interview. Find the answer to the following question.

How does Liane, the interviewer, feel about working at home?

B. **LISTENING FOR MAIN IDEAS**

Listen to the interview again. The interview has been divided into four parts. You will hear a beep at the end of each part. A word or phrase has been given to help you focus on the main idea of each part. Write the main idea in a complete sentence. You should have four statements that make a summary of the interview. Compare your summary with that of another student.

Part 1 fusion

_____

_____

Part 2 blurring lines

_____

_____

Part 3 boundaries

_____

_____

Part 4 refuge

_____

_____

C. LISTENING FOR DETAILS

Read the statements for Part 1. Listen to Part 1 of the interview again and fill in the blanks with the missing information. Do the same for Parts 2–4. Compare your answers with those of another student.

Part 1

1. The interviewer, Liane, has turned her daughter's bedroom into a
   _____ _____.

2. In "What's Happening to Home?" Maggie Jackson explores the issue of balancing work, _____, and _____ in the information age.

3. The fusion of work and home in earlier centuries is illustrated by the fact that many families _____.

Part 2

4. With technology, our bodies can be _____, but our minds are _____.

5. With this fusion of work and home, you have a different relationship with the people at home because your work _____.

6. Maggie Jackson's lines were blurred when she hurried her kids to bed so that she could _____.

7. One positive effect of working at home for Maggie was that she could interview _____ while living on the East coast.

8. The negative effect it had on her was that her work was _____, _____, and _____ into the rest of her house.

Part 3

9. The interviewer says that the advantages of working at home for her are that she can have a cup of coffee, sit in an armchair, and have _____ .

10. The interviewer can _____ to separate her office from the rest of her home to set a physical boundary.

11. Maggie Jackson thinks that boundary-making is _____ and that in this day and age we don't _____ .

Part 4

12. In Olivier Marc's quote, *threshold* does not refer to _____ or _____ .

13. A currency trader in New York has video monitors all around his apartment in order to _____ .

14. More Americans will face the issues of blurred boundaries of work and home as computers and gadgets become _____ and _____ .

15. _____ around the country felt that their home was not a refuge.

D. LISTENING FOR INFERENCE

Listen to the excerpts from the interview and answer the following questions. Compare your answers with those of other students.

Excerpt 1

1. How does the interviewer's personal experience illustrate the theme of blurred boundaries between work and home?

   a. Her daughter moved out of her mother's home to a studio apartment.

   b.   The interview with Maggie Jackson was conducted in the interviewer's home.

   c.   Her technician came to her home to help her conduct an interview with Maggie Jackson in New York.

Excerpt 2

2. How many times do you think Maggie Jackson hurried her kids to bed so she could get back to work?

   a. only once

   b. several times

   c. every night

Excerpt 3

3. What does Liane Hansen think about the boundaries of her new home office?

   a. They have been set physically.

   b. They have been set psychologically.

   c. They have been set both physically and psychologically.

Excerpt 4

4. What does the Olivier Marc quote mean?

   a. The architecture of the home is still important.

   b. Home is a place of comfort and protection.

   c. We are in danger of our work and home life becoming blurred.

IV. ▶ LOOKING AT LANGUAGE

A. USAGE: Adverbial Clauses of Contrast

Notice ▶ Listen to the following examples from the interview. Discuss the purpose of the boldfaced words. Are these ideas the main idea of the speaker?

Examples

1. The fusion of work and home is not a new phenomenon. In earlier centuries, many families lived above the store. But Maggie Jackson says that ***while there are similarities***, there are also major differences.

2. Yes, that was, ***although I can't say it only happened just once***, that was a sort of eureka moment.

Explanation

The boldfaced words are examples of adverbial clauses of contrast. They are used to indicate a contrasting idea to the main idea of the sentence. In the first example, Maggie Jackson believes there are similarities between earlier centuries and today in terms of the fusion of work and home, but she is more interested in the differences. Likewise, in the second example, she is more interested in focusing on the fact that she experienced a "eureka moment" than the fact that her realization happened more than once.

Adverbial clauses of contrast can be written before or after the main idea. For example, Maggie Jackson's statement could also be written as:

> That was a sort of eureka moment, ***although I can't say it only happened just once***.

The following words and phrases can be used to introduce adverbial clauses of contrast:

although	while*
though	despite the fact that
even though	in spite of the fact that

Exercise

Use the phrases in parentheses to combine each pair of statements into one sentence with an adverbial clause of contrast. Consider the ideas expressed in the interview to decide which sentence expresses the main idea and which expresses a contrasting idea. Make sure the contrasting (less important) idea is written as an adverbial clause. Use a comma to separate the adverbial clause of contrast from the main idea.

*use this conjunction to introduce the adverbial clause of contrast at the beginning of the sentence

1. Our minds are in a different place. Our bodies can be home because of technology. (though)

   Though our bodies can be home because of technology, our minds are in a different

   place.

2. Maggie found she was hurrying her kids to bed so that she could get back to work. She could be home to eat dinner, put the kids to bed, and read them a story. (while)

3. Maggie had a lot of flexibility working at home. She found that her work was seeping, leaking, and bleeding into the rest of her house. (although)

4. Liane feels the presence of her office in her house. She loves sitting comfortably at home, drinking coffee, and enjoying the beautiful view. (despite the fact that)

5. Liane Hansen can create a physical boundary by closing the door to her office. She wonders how to create psychological boundaries between work and home. (even though)

6. People are losing the sense of home as a refuge. Technology is helping people create more flexible work situations. (while)

    _____

    _____

    _____

7. Most people who experience the fusion of work and home are in high-tech, high-paying jobs. More people will be facing the issue as technology becomes less expensive. (in spite of the fact that)

    _____

    _____

    _____

B.   PRONUNCIATION: /i/ and /I/

Notice   Listen to the following example from the interview. Notice the tense vowel sound in each of the three highlighted words.

> . . . and I had a lot of flexibility. At the same time I felt as though my work was ***seeping*** and ***leaking*** and ***bleeding*** into the rest of my house.

With a partner, read the three words, exaggerating the pronunciation of the tense vowels (*ee, ea*). Notice that in pronouncing this sound, your lips are spread like in a wide smile.

If you relax the vowel sound of the first two words, what English words do you end up with?

seeping: _____

leaking: _____

Explanation   There are more vowels in English than in most other languages. Consequently, language students often have difficulty differentiating tense and lax vowels. Students often produce a sound that is somewhere in between the two, not tense enough and not lax enough.

In the previous example, the tense /i/ sound is used in the three boldfaced words. This vowel sound receives major stress in these words. If the tense /i/ sound is made lax, it becomes /I/, a different vowel sound in English. Consequently, the word *seeping* becomes *sipping*; the word *leaking* becomes *licking*. These examples show how easily speakers can be misunderstood if they do not make their vowel sounds tense or lax enough. Note how the mouth looks different for the two sounds.

seeping /i/

sipping /I/

Exercise 1

To distinguish the /i/ and /I/ sounds, listen to the following minimal pairs, pairs of words that sound the same except for their vowels. Underline the word you hear. Then circle five minimal pairs to practice reading out loud.

Work with a partner. Take turns reading one word from each of the five minimal pairs you circled. Your partner should write the word he or she hears. Check what your partner has written to verify correct pronunciation and comprehension.

1.	sleep	slip	10.	meat	mitt
2.	Pete	pit	11.	lead	lid
3.	sheep	ship	12.	reason	risen
4.	beat	bit	13.	seat	sit
5.	deed	did	14.	seek	sick
6.	feel	fill	15.	reach	rich
7.	week	wick	16.	feet	fit
8.	cheap	chip	17.	heat	hit
9.	each	itch	18.	least	list

Exercise 2

Work in pairs. Read the following sentences, choosing either the /i/ word or the /I/ word. Your partner will respond with either *a* or *b*, depending on the pronunciation you choose. Change roles and repeat the exercise.

1. You should (leave / live) your life at home!

   a. I can't. My family needs me around!

   b. But my work keeps me in the office most of the day.

2. I need to spend more time at home and try to (feel / fill) my family's needs.

   a. Why don't you know what their needs are?

   b. Do they feel a lack of attention because you spend so much time in the office?

3. The fusion of home and work has (arisen / a reason).

   a. Yes, it's technology!

   b. Yes, we see this phenomenon everywhere now!

4. When Joe announced that he was leaving the office to work at home, his partner presented him with a (fist / feast).

   a. Why was he so angry?

   b. What did they eat to celebrate?

5. With my boss looking over my shoulder all day long, I was less likely to (sleep / slip).

   a. So, now that you work at home, do you make more mistakes?

   b. So, now that you work at home, do you take naps?

6. I can't work in the office anymore because of my awful (fit / feet)!

   a. Why are they in such pain?

   b. Why do you get so angry all the time?

7. Working at home has given Eric more free time. He can now spend more taking care of his family's (sheep / ship).

    a. That's right! They do have a huge boat, don't they?

    b. I didn't know they were farmers.

8. Flexible working hours lead people to (sick / seek) days away from work.

    a. I guess they want to find ways to have more time off.

    b. Why are they more likely to get ill?

V. FOLLOW-UP ACTIVITIES

A. DISCUSSION QUESTIONS

In groups, discuss your answers to the following questions.

1. How can psychological boundaries be set so that the lines between work and home do not become too blurred? Can you offer any suggestions?

2. Discuss the meaning of the following quotes and how they might or might not relate to the fusion of work and home in today's world.

    You can't go home again. (Thomas Wolfe)

    Good-bye, proud world! I'm going home;
    Thou art not my friend and I'm not thine. (Ralph Waldo Emerson)

    Keep the home fires burning,
    While your hearts are yearning;
    Though your lads are far away
    They dream of home.
    There's a silver lining
    Through the dark cloud shining;
    Turn the dark cloud inside out,
    Till the boys come home. (Lena Guilbert Ford)

Mid pleasures and palaces though we may roam,
Be it ever so humble, there's no place like home.   (John Howard Payne)

How does it feel
To be on your own
With no direction home
Like a complete unknown
Like a rolling stone? (Bob Dylan)

Home is the place where
When you go there
They have to take you in. (Robert Frost)

B.   INTERVIEW: Working at Home

1. Take Notes to Prepare

By focusing on Liane Hansen's and Maggie Jackson's experiences and observations, you may be better able to recognize some of the advantages and disadvantages of fusing work and home.

Listen to the interview again. Take notes on details that describe some of the issues involved with the blurring of office and home. Key phrases and an example have been provided for you. Use your notes to help you formulate questions for the interview exercise that follows.

Changes observed when work and home are fused

• A bedroom turns into a mini-studio.

_____

_____

Advantages of the work/home fusion

_____

_____

_____

Disadvantages of the work/home fusion

_____

_____

_____

 2. Interview

Work in pairs. Write six to eight questions for an interview with someone who has combined his or her work and home life. Try to find out how working at home has affected this person's life. Use the topics below to help you prepare your own list of questions. Conduct your interview. You may want to organize your interview so that one person asks the questions and the other takes notes.

- Type of work done at home

- Length of time person has worked at home

- Changes in working at home

- Advantages of working at home

- Disadvantages of working at home

Oral Report

After you conduct your interview, plan an oral report with your partner. Divide your presentation so each of you has a chance to speak. Judge the issue of working at home based on your interviewee's experience.

"What's Happening to Home?" was first broadcast on *All Things Considered*, March 21, 2002. The interviewer is Liane Hansen.

6

Create Controversy
to Generate Publicity

A. PREDICTING

From the title, discuss what you think the interview in this unit is about.

B. THINKING AHEAD

In groups, discuss your answers to the following questions.

1. What makes an advertisement successful? Give examples to explain your answer.

2. Can you think of any companies that have used controversial advertising? What was different about their ads? What reactions did they get from the public?

3. In your opinion, should companies use advertising to promote certain values?

II. ▶ VOCABULARY

Read the following sentences. The boldfaced words will help you understand the interview. Try to determine the meaning of these words from the context. Then write a synonym or your own definition of the words.

1. The Benetton* ad has been ***controversial*** because some people see it as a way to improve race relations while others see it only as a way to sell the company's products.

   _____

2. One of the most important decisions a company must make is how to ***depict*** the company in its advertisements: through photographs, graphic design, illustrations, or other means.

   _____

3. In Catholic schools, ***nuns*** are often classroom teachers.

   _____

4. Bright colors usually ***enhance*** the visual appeal of an advertisement by attracting people's attention.

   _____

5. Companies need people to buy their products, so choosing the best way to increase ***consumer*** exposure to a new product is key to successful advertising.

   _____

6. Magazines are a "natural ***habitat***" for ads; most of the space in magazines is reserved for advertising in order to generate revenue.

   _____

7. Advertisers will sometimes take extreme measures to create an ***arresting*** ad, one that is sure to get the public's attention.

   _____

*United Colors of Benetton

8. It's best not to ask people about their marriages if they are **touchy** about discussing their personal lives.

   _____

9. Advertising is generally used to attract people to a product, not to **tick** them **off** or get them upset about an issue.

   _____

10. Focusing on world issues rather than on the cost of a product is a **cunning** method of advertising.

    _____

11. One **rational** way to save money is to shop less frequently.

    _____

Now match the words in the left column with a definition or synonym in the right column.

_____	1. controversial	a. overly sensitive
_____	2. depict	b. describe; represent in a picture or words
_____	3. nuns	c. sneaky; sly
_____	4. enhance	d. make angry
_____	5. consumer	e. reasonable; logical
_____	6. habitat	f. a person who buys products
_____	7. arresting	g. add to; increase in beauty or value
_____	8. touchy	h. place where something lives or exists; a place where something is usually found
_____	9. tick off	i. striking; holding the attention of someone
_____	10. cunning	j. women who belong to a group of Christian women who serve God
_____	11. rational	k. creating argument

III. LISTENING

A. TASK LISTENING

Listen to the interview. Find the answer to the following question.

How much does a cotton T-shirt cost at Benetton?

B. LISTENING FOR MAIN IDEAS

Listen to the interview again. The interview has been divided into four parts. You will hear a beep at the end of each part. Answer the question for each part in a complete sentence. You should have four statements that make a summary of the interview. Compare your summary with that of another student.

Part 1   What has Benetton done that has caused controversy?

_____

_____

Part 2   How do the Benetton ads help the company?

_____

_____

Part 3   How do the views of the newborn-baby ad differ?

_____

_____

Part 4   According to Bob Garfield, what two purposes do these ads have?

_____

_____

C. **LISTENING FOR DETAILS**

Read the questions for Part 1. Then listen to Part 1 again. As you listen, circle the best answer. Compare your answers with those of another student. If you disagree, listen again.

> **Part 1**

1. Which of the following is *not* true about the magazine advertising business?

    a. The magazine business is doing very well.

    b. Magazines are not publishing as many ads.

    c. Magazines are turning down controversial ads.

2. Which of the following does *not* describe one of the Benetton ads?

    a. a nun kissing a priest

    b. a newborn baby

    c. a little black boy kissing a little blonde white girl

3. Why is Garfield being interviewed?

    a. He is an advertising critic for a magazine.

    b. He works for Benetton.

    c. He called to express his opinions.

Repeat the same procedure for Parts 2–4.

> **Part 2**

4. Why does Garfield think Benetton has produced these ads?

    a. to put Garfield on the radio for an interview

    b. to generate publicity

    c. to place Benetton ads into a new habitat

5. How does Garfield think people probably react when they see the ad with the picture of the newborn baby?

    a. casually

    b. not seriously

    c. angrily

Part 3

6. Which description does Garfield think Benetton would use to describe the newborn baby?

   a. arresting

   b. disgusting

   c. magnificent

7. In discussing the newborn baby, what does Garfield imagine in an ad?

   a. a large intestine

   b. a middle-aged person

   c. a fashion model

Part 4

8. Which magazine published the ad with the newborn baby?

   a. *Essence*

   b. *Self*

   c. *Cosmo*

9. How does the interviewer react to the magazines?

   a. She is surprised they didn't publish the ads.

   b. She objects to their double-page ads.

   c. She thinks they are too skinny.

10. What did Benetton expect to happen with these ads?

    a. It expected most magazines to publish them.

    b. It expected the picture of the newborn baby to become popular.

    c. It expected that its customers would get angry.

11. Why does Garfield think Benetton's advertising is cunning?

    a. It causes the company to actually lose publicity.

    b. It creates a distraction.

    c. It helps consumers pay attention to prices.

12. What does Garfield say about Benetton's prices?

   a. They are rational.

   b. Their cotton T-shirts are reasonably priced.

   c. Their cardigan sweaters are too expensive.

D. LISTENING FOR INFERENCE

Listen to the excerpts from the interview and answer the following questions. Compare your answers with those of other students.

Excerpt 1

1. How would Garfield most likely describe the picture?

   a. arresting

   b. disgusting

   c. magnificent and natural

Excerpt 2

2. Why does Garfield talk about using a picture of a large intestine?

   a. He thinks it would be a more natural ad than that of the newborn baby.

   b. He would like to see one in a fashion magazine.

   c. He wants to show that the Benetton ads have gone too far.

Excerpt 3

3. How does Garfield feel about what Benetton is doing?

   a. He admires their advertising and their pricing.

   b. He admires their advertising, but not their pricing.

   c. He admires neither their advertising nor their pricing.

IV. LOOKING AT LANGUAGE

A. USAGE: Descriptive Adjectives

Notice

Work in groups. Listen to the following examples from the interview. Focus on the boldfaced words. How do they add to the meaning of the speaker's message?

Examples

1. I think that if you . . . uh . . . if you were paging through a magazine and you saw this picture, you would stop cold, even if you'd never heard of the ad or Benetton, because it is such an ***arresting*** picture, this baby.

2. Well, it is that, . . . uh, arresting, some would say ***disgusting***. And I suppose the Benetton people would say that it's ***magnificent*** and ***natural***.

3. It's really very ***cunning*** advertising, Linda, for a lot of reasons.

4. It's ***distracting***, because, rather than focus on trying to come up with some sort of rational benefit for buying a $49 dollar cotton T-shirt, which Benetton knows is not a rational kind of consumer behavior, they're kind of playing a little three-card monte in creating a distraction over here so you won't pay attention to the facts of the matter over on the other side, the facts of the matter being that a $119 cardigan sweater is not a particularly good buy.

Explanation

Descriptive adjectives enhance the meaning of the surrounding text. Many descriptive adjectives were used in this discussion of Benetton's ads. It is helpful in both speaking and writing to use these adjectives.

Exercise

Work in pairs. Brainstorm descriptive words that have meanings similar to and different from words that were used in the interview. Write as many synonyms and antonyms that you can think of for each adjective in the chart on the next page. Compare your lists with other students.

	SYNONYMS	ANTONYMS
arresting		
disgusting		
magnificent		
natural		
cunning		
distracting		

B. PRONUNCIATION: Thought Groups

Notice

Listen to the following example from the interview. Why do you think the groups of words below have been linked? How does the speaker say these words?

The three controversial ads depict a very young nun kissing a priest, a newborn baby only seconds old, and a little blonde white girl next to a little black boy whose hair is fashioned into something that looks a little bit like horns.

Explanation

When we speak, we group words together and join the groups into sentences. The groups are called "thought groups." They help the listener organize the meaning of the sentence.

When reading text, it is often easy to see a thought group. Punctuation such as commas and periods shows us where thought groups begin and end.

Bob Garfield, an advertising critic, was interviewed.

Although there are no rules for how to form thought groups in speaking, we naturally pause when whole ideas are expressed, usually after prepositional phrases, noun phrases, and verb phrases.

	Bob Garfield	will be interviewed	on tomorrow's program.
NOT	Bob Garfield will	be interviewed on	tomorrow's program.

Pausing between different groups of words can change the meaning of a sentence. Notice the different meanings for the following sentence. In the first example, Linda is a popular person; her job is station reporter. In the second example, Linda is a reporter on a radio station that is popular.

Linda Wertheimer is a popular radio station reporter.

Linda Wertheimer is a popular radio station reporter.

Exercise 1

Listen to the following examples from the interview. Some punctuation has been removed. Draw a curved line under the thought groups that you hear in each sentence.

1. What do nuns and priests and newborns and little toddlers blonde and black have to do with selling T-shirts?

2. Well it is that arresting some would say disgusting and I suppose the Benetton people would say that it's magnificent and natural.

3. *Essence* and *Child* magazines did not take the ad with the two children *Self* which published the baby refused the nun *Cosmo* decided it did not see itself with a newborn baby in its pages.

4. Not only is there the publicity benefit they also are a great example of what I call distraction marketing.

Exercise 2

With a partner, practice hearing changes in meaning with different thought groups.
Student A reads either *a* or *b* in the left column. Student B responds with either *a* or *b*
in the right column to show understanding. Switch roles after item 4.

Student A   **Student B**

1. a. Linda thought the newborn baby   a. She thought the picture was
      covered in blood was a pretty   attractive and striking.
      arresting picture.

   b. Linda thought the newborn baby   b. She thought the picture was quite
      covered in blood was a pretty,   striking.
      arresting picture.

2. a. One picture depicts a light blonde   a. The girl has light skin and blonde
      girl kissing a black boy.   hair.

   b. One picture depicts a light, blonde   b. The girl's hair is very blonde.
      girl kissing a black boy.

3. a. I need to pick up some tea,   a. There are two things to pick up.
      shirts, and printer paper.

   b. I need to pick up some   b. There are three things to pick up.
      T-shirts and printer paper.

4. a. "Bob," said Linda, "is impressed by   a. Linda is impressed.
      Benetton's ads."

   b. Bob said, "Linda is impressed by   b. Bob is impressed.
      Benetton's ads."

Now switch roles. A becomes B and B becomes A.

Student B   **Student A**

5. a. The photographer needed to take a   a. He needed to use bright lights to
      bright-light photo for the ad.   take the picture.

   b. The photographer needed to take a   b. The photo needed to be bright,
      bright, light photo for the ad.   not dark.

6. a. The models will need sun, glasses, and   a. The photo can't be taken on
      swimsuits for this photo ad.   a rainy day.

   b. The models will need sunglasses and   b. The models will wear glasses for
      swimsuits for this photo ad.   the photo.

7. a. I saw two new Benetton ads with little boys and little girls.

   a. One ad had boys. The other ad had girls.

  b. I saw two new Benetton ads . . . with little boys, and little girls.

   b. There were two ads. They both had boys and girls in them.

8. a. He recently took a businessday trip for *Advertising Age*.

   a. He left on a Monday, Tuesday, Wednesday, Thursday, or Friday.

  b. He recently took a business day-trip for *Advertising Age*.

   b. He came home the same evening.

V. ▷ FOLLOW-UP ACTIVITIES

A. DISCUSSION QUESTIONS

In groups, discuss your answers to the following questions.

1. Do you agree with Garfield's comment that Benetton's ads are an example of "distraction marketing"? Is the purpose of these ads to distract customers from the high prices of Benetton clothing? Can you think of other examples of distraction marketing?

2. Many companies, including Benetton, give some of their profits to charity. Benetton has remarked that this money can often be spent in ways that do not change society. They claim that their ads sometimes contribute more to society by creating awareness about an issue. Do you agree or disagree?

B. VALUES CLARIFICATION: Magazine Advertisements

1. Take Notes to Prepare

By focusing on Benetton's purpose behind its ads, the public reaction to these ads, and other magazines' publishing decisions, you may be better able to clarify your values in the exercise that follows.

Listen to the interview again. Take notes on Benetton's advertising and the effect it has had on the public. Key phrases and an example have been provided for you. Use your notes to help you in the values clarification exercise that follows.

Benetton's purpose behind the ads

• *create controversy and generate publicity*

Public reaction to the ads

Other magazines' publishing decisions for Benetton ads

✔ 2. **Values Clarification**

Imagine that you are part of the advertising team of *Life* magazine. You have traditionally carried advertisements for clothing manufacturers, including Benetton. In fact, Benetton ads bring a lot of money to your magazine.

There has been some controversy over Benetton's ads and, in the past, some magazines have refused to run them. You must decide which Benetton ads, if any, you will run in your magazine.

Work in groups. Examine the proposed ads on pages 85–86. Use adjectives from Looking at Language on pages 79–81 to describe your reactions to the ads. Decide which of the ads you will consider publishing. Rank your choices from most favorable (1) to least favorable (6). Try to reach a group consensus.

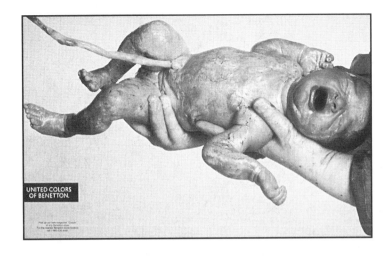

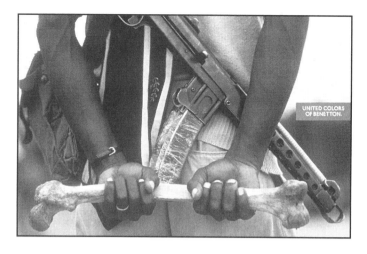

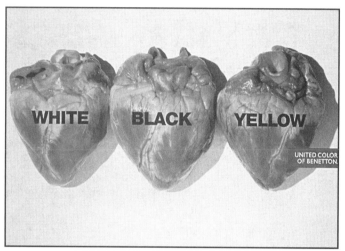

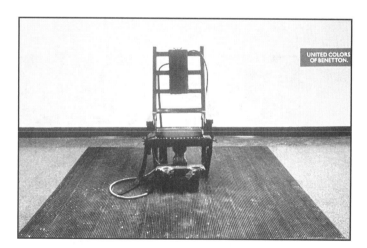

"Create Controversy to Generate Publicity" was first broadcast on *All Things Considered*, September 30, 1991. The interviewer is Linda Wertheimer.

7

A Contribution to Make the
World a Better Place

Financier and philanthropist, George Soros

I. ANTICIPATING THE ISSUE

A. PREDICTING

From the title, discuss what you think the interview in this unit is about.

B. THINKING AHEAD

In groups, discuss your answers to the following questions.

1. People dream of being wealthy. But, what disadvantages can you imagine there might be to having a lot of money?

2. If you had a lot of money, what would you want to do with it?

3. How would you like to be remembered by others?

II. VOCABULARY

Read the text. The boldfaced words will help you understand the interview. Try to determine the meaning of these words. Write the number of each word next to its definition or synonym in the list at the end of the text.

In 1930, George Soros was born in Hungary. His father was a lawyer who liked living well, and Soros was raised in a comfortable, intellectual environment. But his life as a Hungarian Jew became difficult when the Nazis occupied Hungary. Assuming a false identity, Soros learned to survive on the street by dealing with ***black marketers*** who gave him his first lessons in learning the value of things. Amazingly, young George got through this difficult period ***unscathed***, and he looks back on his youth with fond memories.

George Soros went to England in 1947 and attended the London School Economics in 1952. It was there that he became aware of the sad condition of immigrants through his own experiences as an immigrant. While in England, Soros became familiar with the philosopher Karl Popper. Popper had a big influence on Soros's thinking and on his decisions about donating money as a ***philanthropist***.

Soros then moved to the United States in 1956 to become one of the world's biggest ***financiers*** of all time. In America, he began to build a large fortune as an institutional investor. By investing money in organizations or companies, such as banks and insurance companies, and by taking risks investing in ***hedge funds***, his own ***portfolio*** grew larger and larger. Soon Soros became a ***multibillionaire*** and one of the most influential men in the world.

Soros recalls his earlier life saying, "I have prospered, but I know we all need a helping hand at some time in our lives." He established his first foundation, the Open Society Fund, in New York in 1979, his first European foundation in Hungary in 1984, and the Soros Foundation in the Soviet Union in 1987. He now funds a network of foundations that operate in 31 countries; these foundations

allocate money toward the building and maintaining of the basic systems and
8
institutions of a free society. The responsibility he has assumed for others gives
him a lot of influence, but it also gives him worries. He has even experienced
psychosomatic illnesses from managing other people's money.
9

Today, as a philosopher who has traded many *commodities* in the world,
10
Soros talks and writes about the *perils* that could harm the world's economy. He
11
believes that the world is in the middle of financial and political crisis. Soros
points out that there are many *dents* in today's global capitalist system. For
12
example, international financial markets have been the main cause of failing
economies. Consequently, capitalism has many *drawbacks*. However, Soros's
13
work is focused on improving the operation of free markets to protect our
capitalistic societies.

_____ a. relating to the relationship between the mind and physical illness

_____ b. not hurt by a bad or dangerous situation

_____ c. imperfections

_____ d. a collection of stocks owned by a particular person or company

_____ e. rich person who gives money to people who are poor or who need
money to do useful things

_____ f. products that are bought and sold

_____ g. decide to give a particular amount of money

_____ h. an extremely rich person who has many billions of dollars

_____ i. great dangers

_____ j. investment companies that use high risk techniques in order to make
a lot of money

_____ k. people who control or lend large sums of money

_____ l. significant, negative effects

_____ m. people who buy and sell goods illegally

III. LISTENING

A. TASK LISTENING

Listen to the interview. Find the answer to the following question.

How old was George Soros when he first started trading in currency?

B. LISTENING FOR MAIN IDEAS

Listen to the interview again. The interview has been divided into five parts. You will hear a beep at the end of each part. A word or phrase has been given to help you focus on the main idea of each part. Write the main idea in a complete sentence. You should have five statements that make a summary of the interview. Compare your summary with that of another student.

Part 1 multibillionaire

_____

_____

Part 2 anxious

_____

_____

Part 3 experiences in trading

_____

_____

Part 4   feelings about money

_____

_____

Part 5   goal

_____

_____

C.   LISTENING FOR DETAILS

Read the questions for Part 1. Then listen to Part 1 again. As you listen, circle the best answer. Compare your answers with those of another student. If you disagree, listen again.

Part 1

1. What is special about Tuesdays on *Morning Edition*?

    a. The program will discuss taxes.

    b. The program will focus on money.

    c. The program will interview rich people.

2. How is George Soros described?

    a.   one of the world's worthiest men

    b.   a financier

    c.   a philosopher

3. Which of the following is *not* true about Soros?

    a. He is still working.

    b. He ran a hedge fund.

    c. He bought stocks and bonds.

Repeat the same procedure for Parts 2–5.

Part 2

4. What's the problem with managing people's money, according to Soros?

    a. You can't take risks with someone else's money.

    b. You can lose people's money.

    c. People will wake you up at night to see how their portfolio is doing.

5. What negative effect might Soros's currency trading have caused, according to Stamberg?

    a. a stock market crash on Wall Street

    b. Asia's financial crisis.

    c. more financial lies from companies

6. Which of the following is *not* true about Soros's background?

    a. He was born in Budapest.

    b. His father was a lawyer.

    c. He became an economist.

Part 3

7. Which of the following is true about the 14-year-old George Soros?

    a. He assumed a Jewish identity.

    b. He lived underground, or in secret.

    c. He was suspected of carrying currency.

8. What lesson did George learn when he tried to trade?

    a. Sellers' estimates were usually reliable.

    b. His merchandise was full of dents and not worth anything.

    c. Gold was a commodity whose price could change.

9. How did young George feel about his experiences?

    a. They were frightening.

    b. They were a gift.

    c. Fighting evil made him suffer.

Part 4

10. Which of the following describes George Soros's background?

    a. He fought the Communists.

    b. He left Hungary in 1956.

    c. He arrived in America with $4,000 in his pocket.

11. Which of the following describes George Soros's "plan?"

    a. He would make a million dollars on Wall Street in five years.

    b. He would live on $15,000 a year.

    c. He would become a philosopher.

12. How would Soros have liked to be appreciated by others?

    a. as a person who could make a lot of money

    b. as a thinker

    c. as someone who was knowledgeable about the stock market

13. What fascinates Soros?

    a. the pursuit of money

    b. the anticipation of the future

    c. what money can buy

14. What does having money allow Soros to do?

    a. focus on buying expensive things

    b. buy a private plane and boat

    c. pursue his ideas

Part 5

15. How does Soros react to the idea that he is "saving the world"?

    a. He rejects it totally.

    b. He thinks it's very amusing.

    c. He agrees with it.

16. Which of the following is *not* correct in terms of numbers?

a. His foundations allocate half a billion dollars a year.

b. His foundations allocate money to 30 countries.

c. He has changed the lives of thousands of people.

17. How does Soros feel about giving money?

a. He doesn't like to give money to beggars on the street.

b. He seeks personal gratitude.

c. He likes meeting the people who have received his money.

18. How would George Soros like to be remembered?

a. as an author who has contributed to the world of finance

b. as a practical financier

c. as a philosopher trying to understand life

D. LISTENING FOR INFERENCE

Listen to the excerpts from the interview and answer the following questions. Compare your answers with those of other students.

Excerpt 1

1. Why does Stamberg say that Wall Street would have sent Soros for X-rays?

_____

_____

Excerpt 2

2. What does Stamberg imply by her comment about Soros's father?

_____

_____

Excerpt 3

3. Why does Stamberg emphasize Soros's eye and hair color in her comment?

_____

_____

IV.   LOOKING AT LANGUAGE

A.   USAGE: Past Unreal Conditional

Notice

Listen to the following example from the interview. Notice the boldfaced verb forms in the statement. Is the speaker talking about the present or the past?

> Imagine if Wall Street **had known** that. They**'d have sent** him for daily X-rays.

Explanation

In the example above, the interviewer is imagining an unreal situation in the past. She imagines an unreal condition and an unreal result of that condition. This statement can also be read as:

> Imagine if Wall Street **had known** that. They **would have sent** him for daily X-rays.

The past unreal conditional is generally formed as follows:

Condition clause	Result clause
_If_ + subject + (not) past perfect tense	subject + _would/could/might (not) have_ + _past participle_
If Wall Street **had known** about Soros's backaches,	they **would/could/might have sent** him for daily X-rays.
If Soros **had not had** backaches,	he **would/could/might not have known** that there was something wrong with his portfolio.

Exercise

Complete the sentences, using information from the interview with George Soros.
Use the past unreal conditional in each sentence.

1. If George Soros had not been responsible for other people's money,

   <u>he wouldn't have had anxiety and backaches.</u>

2. If the Nazis had not invaded Hungary when George was a young boy, _____

   _____

3. _____ ,

   it could have been more dangerous for young George to trade in currency.

4. If Soros had not accomplished his five-year plan, _____

   _____

5. _____ ,

   George Soros wouldn't have been able to pursue his ideas.

6. _____ ,

   he would not have created foundations that allocate half a billion dollars a year.

B.   PRONUNCIATION: Word Stress for Meaning Differentiation

Notice   Listen to the following example from the interview. Focus on word stress in
different parts of this exchange. As you listen to the excerpt, mark the
stressed word with a stress mark (′) in:

  • the second sentence of Soros's comment.

  • Stamberg's question.

  • the second sentence of Soros's answer.

SOROS: I don't need to be concerned how much something costs. <u>For instance, I don't need to have a private plane.</u>

STAMBERG: <u>You don't have a private plane?</u>

SOROS: I don't have a private plane. <u>I don't need to have a private plane.</u>

With a partner, discuss how word stress affects meaning in the examples above.

Explanation

When a word in a sentence is emphasized, it gives information about a speaker's meaning. The same sentence can have different meanings when different words are stressed. Usually, the word that is stressed in a sentence is louder, higher in pitch and longer (the vowel is lengthened).

In the first example above, Soros focuses on *plane*. He may need other private things, but he emphasizes that he does not need a plane, as many other rich people may feel they do. In Stamberg's question, she emphasizes *don't*, making sure that she has understood Soros correctly. She seems to be surprised by the fact that he doesn't actually have a private plane. In the last example, Soros emphasizes that he has no *need* for a private plane, even though he can certainly afford one.

Exercise 1

How does the meaning change when other words in Stamberg's question are stressed? Match each question with the response that best fits its meaning, based on the word stress.

_____ 1. **You** don't have a private plane?   a. So, you must borrow a private plane from a friend.

_____ 2. You don't **have** a private plane?   b. So, you must have a private boat.

_____ 3. You don't have **a** private plane?   c. I would have thought that a rich man like you would have one.

_____ 4. You don't have a **private** plane?   d. You must have more than one.

_____ 5. You don't have a private **plane**?   e. Do you share your plane with a friend?

Work in pairs. Student A reads the questions above out of order, stressing the boldfaced words. After each question, Student B responds with the corresponding comment to show he or she has understood the word stress.

Exercise 2

With a partner, practice meaning differentiation with different word stress. Student A reads either *a* or *b* in the left column. Student B responds with either *a* or *b* in the right column to show understanding. Switch roles after item 3.

Student A	**Student B**
1. a. Is Soros a wealthy woman?	a. Actually, he is one of the world's wealthiest ***men***.
b. Is Soros one of the nation's wealthiest men?	b. Actually, he is one of the ***world's*** wealthiest men.
2. a. Did Soros speculate in commodities?	a. No, he speculated in ***currencies***.
b. Did Soros trade in many currencies?	b. No, he ***speculated*** in currencies.
3. a. Didn't George Soros use to get a lot of backaches?	a. Yes, and he ***gave*** a lot of backaches to people, too.
b. Did Soros give a lot of money to people?	b. Yes, and he gave a lot of ***backaches*** to people, too.

Now switch roles. A becomes B and B becomes A.

Student B	**Student A**
4. a. Did Soros's money lead to Asia's financial success?	a. In fact, Soros's money may have contributed to Asia's financial ***crisis***.
b. Did Soros's money lead to the the Soviet Union's financial crisis?	b. In fact, Soros's money may have contributed to ***Asia's*** financial crisis.
5. a. When did Soros have blonde hair?	a. When Soros was a ***kid***, he had blonde hair.
b. What color hair did Soros have when he was young?	b. When Soros was a kid, he had ***blonde*** hair.
6. a. Is Soros usually thought of as a thinker?	a. He wants to be thought of as a ***thinker.***
b. Is Soros usually thought of as a multibillionaire?	b. He ***wants*** to be thought of as a thinker.

V. FOLLOW-UP ACTIVITIES

A. DISCUSSION QUESTIONS

In groups, discuss your answers to the following questions.

1. Why does George Soros say he doesn't need a private plane or boat? What needs does he have? Why do you think he says this?

2. What kind of life experiences help people toward success? Consider the life of George Soros and discuss any of his life experiences that seem to be common among successful people.

B.   VALUES CLARIFICATION: The Values of a Philanthropist

1. Take Notes to Prepare

By focusing on George Soros's life experiences, you may be better able to react to the importance of his foundations' projects.

Listen to the interview again. Take notes on experiences from Soros's life that may have led to his role as a philanthropist. Key phrases and an example have been provided for you. Use your notes to help you in the values clarification exercise that follows.

Soros's physical effects from handling other people's money

• made him anxious _____

_____

_____

_____

_____

His life as a 14-year-old boy

_____

_____

_____

_____

_____

Coming to America

_____

_____

_____

_____

_____

His personal values today:

What he wants

_____

_____

_____

What he doesn't want

_____

_____

_____

✓ 2. **Values Clarification**

Work in groups. Read the following project descriptions of the Soros Foundation's U.S. Programs. Consider the purpose and goal of each project. Based on the interview with Soros, which of these projects best reflects Soros's values? If you were George Soros, to which projects would you allocate the most money? Rank these choices from the one you think most reflects Soros's goals (1) to the one you think reflects them the least (5).

Then, consider the problems of your communities. Decide which of these projects are most important and would deserve the most financial support.

_____ **Criminal Justice Initiative**

The goals of this initiative are to reduce unnecessary dependence on the use of prisons and to promote equal and fair treatment in the criminal justice system. The initiative includes programs which: 1) help prisoners reenter their communities, 2) explore alternative systems of punishment, 3) find ways to put an end to the death penalty, and 4) provide education to prisoners.

_____ Youth Initiatives

These programs are focused on helping disadvantaged youth, especially those who often experience racism and poverty. The goal of these programs is to open up opportunities for young people to gain skills and compete in the modern world. The three programs consist of: 1) The Arts Initiative, which aims to increase access to the arts for all people, 2) The Urban Debate Program, which teaches students to debate controversial topics, and 3) The Youth Media and Communications Program, which supports the involvement of minorities in media.

_____ Emma Lazarus Fund

This fund supports nonprofit organizations that help legal immigrants become U.S. citizens as well as organizations that provide legal service to immigrants. One goal of this program is to fight anti-immigrant attitudes in the U.S. Another is to ensure equal protection by the government, such as in making sure legal immigrants receive their share of welfare benefits. Ninety percent of the fund is used to help legal immigrants become citizens.

_____ Project on Death in America

The goal of this project is to transform the culture of dying. Money from this project is used to improve care for the terminally ill and their families. It is also used to educate the public about the difficult issues surrounding death and dying. For example, projects focus on: 1) improving doctor-patient communication about end-of-life issues, 2) developing care for the dying in nursing homes, 3) providing homecare for children dying of AIDS, and 4) providing information on physician-assisted suicide.

_____ Soros Documentary Fund

Money from this fund is used to support documentary films and videos that deal with human rights, freedom of expression and social liberties. Here are some examples of recently funded films:

Children Underground reveals the lives of abandoned children who live in subways below the streets in Bucharest, Romania.

I Was A Slave Labourer is about the current campaign for justice, recognition, and compensation by former slave-laborers of the Nazi industrial and economic complex.

The Charcoal People portrays the thousands of migrant workers who cut down forests in the Brazilian Amazon to produce charcoal for steel industries in Brazil and abroad.

900 Women: Inside St. Gabriel's Prison documents the lives of six women who live in the largest jail in Louisiana. They survive giving birth while facing many challenges and the possibility of dying in prison.

"A Contribution to Make the World a Better Place" was first broadcast on *Morning Edition*, April 3, 2001. The interviewer is Susan Stamberg.

8

Medicine by the Minute

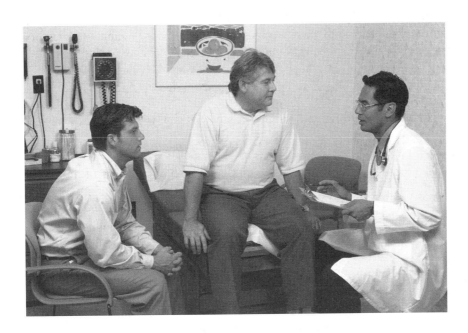

A. PREDICTING

From the title, discuss what you think the interview in this unit is about.

B. THINKING AHEAD

In groups, discuss your answers to the following questions.

1. If you have to visit the doctor, who pays—you or your health insurance? How does it work?

2. What kind of services do you expect when you visit a doctor? What kind of services do you usually get?

3. Describe the state of health insurance where you live. Are people generally happy or unhappy with their services?

II. VOCABULARY

Read the text. The boldfaced words will help you understand the interview. Try to determine the meaning of these words. Write the number of each word next to its definition or synonym in the list at the end of the text.

When most Americans go to the doctor, the first thing they are usually asked is not what's wrong with them but what kind of insurance they have. In some cases, patients are now asked to pay their **co-pay**, even before seeing the doctor! Doctors want to be sure that patients will pay their share of the fee before requesting the insurance payment. In today's world, doctors, medical office workers, and patients are consumed by the administration of managed care, a system of healthcare that has become very common in the United States. Under this system, patients have insurance that allows them to use only particular doctors or hospitals and sometimes limits the kinds of medicine, tests, or procedures that they can get.

In managed care, doctors have to fill out a lot of insurance forms and follow many rules so that insurance companies will pay them for a patient's treatment. With the added time required to argue with insurance companies so that patients' bills can be paid, **primary care** doctors have been forced to cut back on patient care. Some doctors may now be required to see up to eight patients in an hour to make up for the time and money lost with paperwork.

Many doctors and patients have "had it." They are **fed up with** this system and would like to see a change. They think medicine doesn't work when business controls the medical world. In fact, some doctors are beginning to leave the system, even when they will make only half of their salary. For example, some doctors are opening up their own **acute care** clinics. Instead of accepting insurance and dealing with all the administrative headaches, they give patients an **itemized** bill and ask to be paid in cash at the end of each visit. So, like a car **mechanic** who charges for labor and parts, an **osteopath** who sees a patient for a back injury might charge for his or her time and the individual medical supplies used in treatment.

These clinics offer a relief to patients, as well. Instead of spending days waiting to see their primary physician for a small ***bruise*** or cut, patients can now walk in and see a doctor in 10 to 15 minutes, and they can have more immediate and personal contact with a doctor. Often, the price a patient pays for this service is not much higher than an insurance co-pay. He may have to pay for the ***suture tray*** because the doctor's instruments need to be ***sterilized*** after use. He may have to pay for an ***injection*** because the doctor has to ***anesthetize*** him. But in the end, the expenses are generally the same as the co-pay required by insurance companies.

Cash-only clinics may be the way of the future as people become more and more dissatisfied with the managed healthcare system.

_____ a. main source of medical care provided by one's insurance company

_____ b. with all the parts listed

_____ c. a doctor who treats muscles and bones

_____ d. the act of giving a drug through a needle

_____ e. tray with material for sewing a wound

_____ f. someone who is skilled at repairing motor vehicles and machinery

_____ g. medical care for people with severe injuries or illnesses that need help urgently

_____ h. give a drug to stop a person from feeling pain

_____ i. fee paid by insured patients for doctor's visit

_____ j. purple or brown mark on your skin from a fall or hit

_____ k. completely cleaned from any bacteria

_____ l. tired of

III. ▶ LISTENING

A. TASK LISTENING

Listen to the interview. Find the answer to the following question.

Where did Lisa Grigg get the ideas for her clinic?

B. LISTENING FOR MAIN IDEAS

Listen to the interview again. The interview has been divided into five parts. You will hear a beep at the end of each part. A word or phrase has been given to help you focus on the main idea of each part. Write the main idea in a complete sentence. You should have five statements that make a summary of the interview. Compare your summary with that of another student.

Part 1   clinic

_____

_____

Part 2   charge

_____

_____

Part 3   simple

_____

_____

> **Part 4**   acute care

_____

_____

> **Part 5**   off-the-clock

_____

_____

C.   LISTENING FOR DETAILS

Read the statements for Part 1. Listen to Part 1 of the interview again and fill in the blanks with the missing information. Do the same for Parts 2–5. Compare your answers with those of another student.

> **Part 1**

1. Lisa Grigg "had it" with insurance _____ and insurance

   _____ .

2. She hung out a shingle* as an _____

   _____ provider.

3. Patients are charged according to a _____ schedule that

   they can easily understand.

> **Part 2**

4. Lisa Grigg charges _____ a minute for labor.

5. In addition to charging for her labor when treating a bruise or cut, Grigg would

   also have to charge for a _____

   _____ and an _____ .

hung out a shingle: opened a new business

6. Her itemized bill would show the charge by the _____ and

   by the _____ .

Part 3

7. Lisa Grigg was feeling _____ _____

   _____ managed care.

8. The problems she had with managed care were that there was an awful

   lot of _____ , an awful lot of tail chasing, and an awful lot of

   _____ with insurances for tests or medicines.

9. Like her mechanic, Lisa Grigg has a _____

   _____ hanging up in her office.

Part 4

10. Average co-pays are between _____ and

    _____ dollars.

11. Lisa Grigg encourages people to stay with their _____

    _____ physicians.

12. At her last job, Lisa Grigg spent about _____ hours a day

    with patients and _____ to _____

    hours a day making phone calls or doing paperwork.

Part 5

13. Robert Siegel wonders if Lisa Grigg has a blanket rule[*] for

    _____ , no matter what the problem is.

14. Lisa Grigg is fairly _____ with her off-the-clock time.

[*] *blanket rule*: general policy

15. If she thinks a _____ is something more serious, then

    she will sit and talk with a patient.

16. Robert thinks Lisa's _____ _____

    must be frustrated with their interview.

LISTENING FOR INFERENCE

Listen to the excerpts from the interview. Try to understand the speaker's attitude by listening to his or her tone of voice and choice of words. Choose the best answer for each question. Compare your answers with those of another student. Listen to the excerpts again if necessary.

Excerpt 1

1. What attitude does Lisa Grigg express in her answers?

   a. one of humor

   b. one of embarrassment

   c. one of confidence

Excerpt 2

2. What attitude does Robert Siegel express in his comment to Lisa Grigg?

   a. one of surprise

   b. one of interest

   c. one of humor

Excerpt 3

3. What attitude does Lisa Grigg express toward paperwork?

   a. one of acceptance

   b. one of annoyance

   c. one of disgust

Excerpt 4

4. What attitude does Robert Siegel express in his question?

    a. one of doubt

    b. one of disbelief

    c. one of humor

IV. LOOKING AT LANGUAGE

A. USAGE: Present Unreal vs. Future Real Conditions

Notice

In the following example, Robert Siegel, the interviewer, imagines that he is a patient at Lisa Grigg's clinic. He presents his scenario as an unreal, imaginary case by using a condition clause with the term *Let's say*, which has the same meaning as "Imagine that . . ." or "If . . ." During the interview, however, the scenario starts to sound like a real case. Can you tell what causes this to happen? How does this change the nature of the conversation?

Listen to the example. Draw a slash (/) at the point where the unreal situation begins to sound like a real situation.

SIEGEL: Let's say I went in with, you know, a bruise or a cut, and you had to bandage me up.

DR. GRIGG: I'd still charge for my labor. I'd have to also charge for a suture tray because my instruments will have to be sterilized after I use them on you. And a little bit for an injection.

SIEGEL: Hmm.

DR. GRIGG: Hoping we want to anesthetize you.

SIEGEL: So I really get an itemized bill here, and I know exactly what I'm paying for.

DR. GRIGG: Right.

SIEGEL: And charge me by the minute and by the part.

DR. GRIGG: Yep.

Explanation

In the previous example, Robert Siegel presents a situation in which he would go to Lisa Grigg's clinic with a bruise or cut. He sees this as a hypothetical, unreal situation.

The present unreal condition is formed as follows:

Condition clause (*If* clause)	Result clause
If + subject + past tense	subject + *would* + base verb
If Robert went to the clinic and **had** to be bandaged up,	**Lisa would charge** him for her labor.

However, in the middle of the conversation, Lisa continues as if the situation were real, and from that point on, the conversation continues in the future real condition. This switch between unreal and real conditions sometimes occurs in everyday conversations.

The future real condition is formed as follows:

Condition clause (*If* clause)*	Result clause
If + subject + past tense	subject + *will* + base verb
If I use a suture tray,	my **instruments will have to be** sterilized after I use them.

Exercise

Complete the sentences with information from the interview. Focus on form for the corresponding *if* clause and result clause. Fill in the blanks with the word given in parentheses using the future real condition or present unreal condition.

1. If a patient comes to Lisa Grigg with a bruise or a cut, she

   _____ (charge) for labor, a suture tray, and an injection.

2. If Robert Siegel _____ (go) to Lisa Grigg's clinic, he would

   be charged by the minute and by the part.

3. If Lisa had more paperwork in her clinic, she _____

   (not / spend) as much time as she does with her patients.

4. If Lisa _____ (accept) co-pay, she would have more

   paperwork.

*This clause can come before or after the result clause.

5. Lisa _____ (tell) her patients to see their primary care physicians if they need more than acute care.

6. Lisa would go off-the-clock if she _____ (feel) a patient had a serious problem.

7. If Lisa gives a lot of off-the-clock time to her patients, her office manager _____ (get) frustrated with her.

B. PRONUNCIATION: Noun Compounds

Notice

Listen to the following example from the interview. Focus on the boldfaced word. Which syllable is stressed?

> I was just feeling fed up with the way the practice I was in was running, which was an owned clinic and doing a lot of managed care and capitated care,* and there was an awful lot of **paperwork** and an awful lot of tail chasing and an awful lot of fighting with insurances for tests or medicines that patients needed, and I just wanted to get back to being a doctor and treating patients.

Explanation

Noun compounds are formed by combining two nouns. Sometimes the nouns are joined together as one word. Sometimes they remain separate. In noun compounds, the first noun is more heavily stressed than the second noun. It is also pronounced on a higher pitch. In the above example, *paper* is more heavily stressed and pronounced on a higher pitch than *work*.

Exercise

Work in pairs. Read the following questions and answers. Student A reads the question, and Student B answers. Be sure to read the noun compounds with the correct stress and pitch. Switch roles after item 5.

1. A: Don't you like that music?

   B: No. It's really giving me a headache. I wish they'd turn it off.

2. A: Why can't you walk?

   B: I fell when I went ice skating and broke my kneecap!

*capitated care: care for which doctors are paid a certain amount of money

3. A: You eat too much spicy food! No wonder you always feel uncomfortable.

    B: I know. I really have to do something about this heartburn.

4. A: That boxer sure looked messy after the fight.

    B: Yeah, and it wasn't his first nosebleed. He's had many!

5. A: What's the matter? You sound awful!

    B: I know I do, but it's only a head cold.

Now switch roles. A becomes B and B becomes A.

6. B: Why do you keep touching your foot?

    A: My toenail fell off and now my foot hurts!

7. B: Why are you holding your arm up in the air?

    A: I hurt myself swimming, and I have a sore armpit.

8. B: What happened to your grandmother? Why does she have to go to the hospital?

    A: She has a problem with her hip joint and fell last week.

9. B: Why do you have so much trouble getting out of bed in the morning?

    A: Because I'm stiff and have a backache from exercising.

10. B: How did your checkup go at the doctor's?

    A: Well, everything is fine, except that he found an irregular heartbeat. He wants me to get it checked again in a month.

V. FOLLOW-UP ACTIVITIES

A. DISCUSSION QUESTIONS

In groups, discuss your answers to the following questions.

1. Would you go to Lisa Grigg's clinic for acute care? Why or why not? If so, in which circumstances would you go to her?

2. Lisa Grigg's story is an example of a person in one line of work becoming more effective by borrowing ideas from a person in another line of work. Can you think of other examples where this has been done? Share stories you know in which a professional used ideas or practices from a different profession to do a better job.

B. CASE STUDY: Dial-a-Doc

1. Take Notes to Prepare

By focusing on Lisa Grigg's frustrations with the current situation in the medical world, the ideas she took from her mechanic, and the policies she set up in her own clinic, you may be better able to evaluate the case study that follows.

Listen to the interview again. Take notes on the Lisa Grigg story. Key phrases and an example have been provided for you.

Payment options

•$2 / minute for labor

_____

_____

_____

_____

_____

Types of patient care/needs

_____

_____

_____

_____

_____

Time with patients

_____

_____

_____

_____

_____

2. Case Study

You have listened to how and why Lisa Grigg opened up her cash-only clinic. In this case, doctors equally frustrated with managed care found a very different solution to providing better patient care.

Work in groups. Read the following case. Then act as a committee that is studying doctors' phone consultations. Make a list of advantages and disadvantages you see with Dial-a-Doc services. Then make a list of rules these doctors must follow. Compare your lists with those of the other groups.

Many doctors and patients, frustrated with managed care and the lack of personal attention doctors are able to give patients these days, are seeking ways people can gain more control over their health. A few years ago, Brent Blue, a medical doctor from Wyoming, established Dial-a-Doc, a service in which people can call up and speak to a doctor within 60 seconds. This is an attractive alternative to the time people usually spend trying to talk to their doctor, which involves scheduling an appointment, driving to the doctor's office, and sitting in the waiting room to see the doctor. Given the fact that 70% of doctors visits are people looking for medical information, this service makes a lot of sense. Dial-a-Doc is available 24 hours a day, 7 days a week and only costs about $2 a minute. The phone doctors are often retired doctors who want to continue working at home without having to travel to an office, attend meetings, or do paperwork. They work 12-hour shifts, evenly split between day and night. They can work a maximum of two shifts (24 hours) in a row.

Most of the calls doctors receive are from mothers who are anxious about their babies, people wondering if they really need to see a doctor, and people concerned about the medications they should or shouldn't be taking. Some people call Dial-a-Doc when they are afraid to ask their own doctor certain questions or when they are looking for a second opinion. Others use Dial-a-Doc for emergencies.

Dial-a-Doc has received a fair amount of criticism. Although the service, and others like it, stresses that it neither diagnoses illness nor prescribes medication, callers often have the perception that they are getting medical care, and they will take any advice they get seriously. Yet, a phone call to a doctor is really just a conversation and not the same as an in-person interview or exam. The doctor and patient never meet. In addition, a research institute that studies consumer health information determined that over-the-phone medical advice is often incomplete and that doctors taking phone calls may be tempted to diagnose a problem rather quickly. Other critics point out that services such a Dial-a-Doc are a simple solution to a larger problem: They worry that, with such services, true healthcare reform may be further delayed.

As patients become more and more frustrated with managed care, this service is likely to become even more popular. Some predict that we may even be entering a new era of "information doctors," in which doctors will specialize in caring for people over the phone. Meanwhile, the American Medical Association is concerned about the usefulness and safety of such care. They are considering rules for call-in doctors.

Advantages and Disadvantages

• Doctors don't examine patients. _____

_____

• Many Dial-a-Doc doctors are _____

retired and may not know about _____

the latest medical research. _____

_____

_____

_____

_____

_____

_____

_____

_____

_____

Rules

• Doctors can't diagnose illnesses _____

or prescribe medicine. _____

_____

_____

_____

_____

_____

_____

_____

_____

_____

_____

"Medicine by the Minute" was first broadcast on *All Things Considered*, April 26, 2000. The interviewer is Robert Siegel.

9

Facing the Wrong End of a Pistol

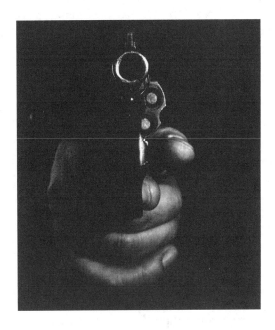

I. ANTICIPATING THE ISSUE

A. PREDICTING

From the title, discuss what you think the interview in this unit is about.

B. THINKING AHEAD

Work in groups. Read the following statements. Do you agree with them?
Does everyone in your group have the same opinion? Discuss.

1. The only purpose of handguns is to kill people.

2. Rifles are acceptable guns because they are primarily used in hunting.

3. Gun manufacturers are responsible for crimes committed with guns.

4. Everyone should have the right to a gun for self-protection.

II. ▷ VOCABULARY

Read the following sentences. The boldfaced words will help you understand the interview. Try to determine the meaning of these words from the context. Then write a synonym or your own definition of the words.

1. Violent criminals use different kinds of weapons. Handguns **account for** many of their crimes.

   _____

2. Some gun manufacturers want to **lift the bans** against sales of some guns because bans have hurt their business.

   _____

3. Some people want to **exempt** certain handguns **from** government proposals that generally support gun sales. These handguns are responsible for many crimes.

   _____

4. Some victims of gun crimes have **launched attacks** against the manufacturers of guns. The victims feel that the manufacturers are responsible for the crimes committed with guns.

   _____

5. Olen Kelley went to his county's court and went before the judge. He **filed suit** against those who he felt were responsible for the crime against him.

   _____

6. Is the maker of a gun responsible for crimes committed with that gun simply because he **manufactures** it?

   _____

7. Two robbers **held up** the bank. They used handguns that were easy to carry and would scare the people in the bank.

   _____

8. Are the companies that sell guns responsible for crimes committed with those guns simply because they ***distribute*** them?

_____

9. The robbers used handguns, but they did not want to hurt people. They ***were*** only ***after*** money.

_____

Now match the words in the left column with a definition or synonym in the right column.

_____ 1. account for   a. not included in

_____ 2. lift a ban   b. bring charges against someone

_____ 3. exempt from   c. sell to stores

_____ 4. launch an attack   d. produce; make

_____ 5. file suit   e. want

_____ 6. manufacture   f. rob with a weapon

_____ 7. hold up   g. remove a rule that says something is bad

_____ 8. distribute   h. fight

_____ 9. be after   i. be responsible for

The following words will help you understand the crime described in the interview. Draw lines to connect the words with the parts of the body they identify.

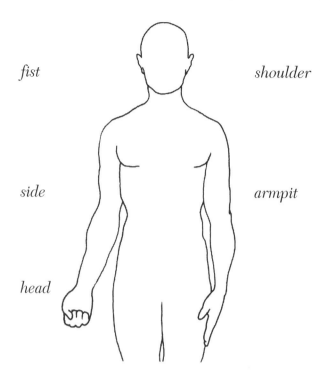

fist

shoulder

side

armpit

head

III. LISTENING

A. TASK LISTENING

Listen to the interview. Find the answer to the following question.

Is Olen Kelley against all guns?

B. LISTENING FOR MAIN IDEAS

Listen to the interview again. The interview has been divided into three parts. You will hear a beep at the end of each part. Answer the question for each part in a complete sentence. You should have three statements that make a summary of the interview. Compare your summary with that of another student.

Part 1   How are some people trying to change gun laws?

_____

_____

Part 2   What happened to Kelley?

_____

_____

Part 3   Who is Kelley suing?

_____

_____

C. LISTENING FOR DETAILS

Read the questions for Part 1. Then listen to Part 1 again. As you listen, circle the best answer. Compare your answers with those of another student. If you disagree, listen again.

Part 1

1. Statistics show that many people will _____.

   a. own a handgun in their lives

   b. be held up in their lives

   c. commit a crime in their lives

2. What change in the Gun Control Act has the Senate Judiciary Committee proposed?

   a. The sale of guns would be banned.

   b. Most bans against the sale of guns across state lines would be lifted.

   c. Only some states would sell guns.

3. Senator Edward Kennedy tried to _____.

   a. increase the sale of Saturday Night Specials

   b. stop the proposal from being passed

   c. stop the sale of Saturday Night Specials

4. Olen Kelley _____.

   a. owns a grocery store

   b. attacked someone

   c. has been held up five times

Repeat the same procedure for Parts 2 and 3.

Part 2

5. What happened when Kelley tried to open the safe the first time?

   a. He couldn't get it open.

   b. He got the money out.

   c. He took his gun.

6. What did the robbers do to Kelley?

   a. They hit him over the head with a gun.

   b. They shot him in the shoulder.

   c. They shot him in the armpit.

Part 3

7. Where is the maker of the gun located?

   a. in Florida

   b. in Rome

   c. in Germany

8. What does Kelley say about knives?

   a. They are meant to kill people.

   b. They are used for purposes other than crime.

   c. They are cheap.

9. Why does Kelley criticize junk guns?

    a. They can't be used for sports.

    b. They are hard to use.

    c. It's difficult to shoot something with them from far away.

10. Which of the following reasons does Kelley give for taking his suit to the Supreme Court,* if necessary?

    a. He has to take it to the Supreme Court.

    b. He has a lot of time.

    c. He feels he has the right to try.

11. What is Kelley's most important goal in taking his case to court?

    a. He wants to make $500 million.

    b. He wants to sue the lawyers.

    c. He wants to stop the manufacturer from making Saturday Night Specials.

D. LISTENING FOR INFERENCE

Listen to the excerpts from the interview. Read the following statements. Decide whether they are true or false, based on the information given. Write *T* or *F* next to each statement. Compare your answers with those of another student. Listen again if necessary.

Excerpt 1

    ___ 1. The interviewer thinks Kelley might have been injured badly.

    ___ 2. The bullet went *out of* and *back into* his body.

Excerpt 2

    ___ 3. Kelley is suing the gun manufacturer.

    ___ 4. Kelley is frustrated that he doesn't know all the legal technicalities.

    ___ 5. Kelley thinks gun manufacturers are responsible for crimes.

---

* *Supreme Court*: the highest court in the United States, with power to change the decisions made by any of the courts in the nation.

Excerpt 3

___ 6. Kelley would sue the knife manufacturer if he were robbed at knifepoint.

___ 7. Kelley would sue the rifle manufacturer if he were robbed at gunpoint with a rifle.

IV. LOOKING AT LANGUAGE

A. USAGE: Present Perfect vs. Simple Past to Express Past Time

Notice

Listen to the introduction to the interview. Notice the grammatical structures of the boldfaced words. Are they similar or different? When did these events occur? What key phrases signal the use of the present perfect or simple past tenses?

> Handguns account for much of the violent crimes in this country. Statistics show that one out of every five of us will face the wrong end of a pistol in our lives. The Senate Judiciary Committee **decided** this week to propose changes in the 1968 Gun Control Act that would lift most bans against the sales of guns across state lines. During the debate Senator Edward Kennedy **tried**, but **failed**, to exempt the guns known as "Saturday Night Specials" from the proposal. Olen Kelley, a grocery store manager from Silver Spring, Maryland, **has launched** his own attack against Saturday Night Specials. He's **filed** suit in his home county's circuit court to try to stop the manufacture and distribution of the cheap handguns. Kelley **has been held up** more than once; each time the robber **had** a gun. A year ago he **was held up** for the fifth time by two men who were after the money in the store's safe.

Explanation

The present perfect tense is used to describe something that happened before now, at an unspecified time in the past. The exact time it happened is unknown or not important. Often the adverbs *ever*, *never*, *already*, *yet*, *still*, and *just* are seen with this usage of the present perfect.

The present perfect tense is also used to express the repetition of an activity before now. Again, the exact time of each repetition is not important.

The simple past tense is used when there *is* a specific mention of time. Notice the time phrases, *this week*, *during the debate*, *each time*, and *a year ago* in the previous example. In these cases, the simple past is used because there is a clear time reference.

Notice the form of the present perfect and simple past tenses:

Present perfect   **Simple past**

have + past participle   base verb + *-ed*
                                       (many verbs have irregular past forms)

TENSE	EXAMPLE	MEANING
Present perfect	Maryland **has launched** its own attack against Saturday Night Specials. Kelley **has been held up** more than once.	It happened at an unspecified time in the past. This has happened more than one time. The exact time is not important; the repetition of the event is.
Simple past	The Senate Judiciary Committee **decided** this week to propose changes in the 1968 Gun Control Act.	The time of the event is clear. It happened this week.

Exercise

Read the following sentences. Use the context of each sentence to determine whether the present perfect tense or simple past tense best completes the sentence. Fill in the blank with the correct form of the verb in parentheses. Some sentences include negative forms and/or passive voice.

1. One out of every five people _____ (face) the wrong end

   of a pistol in his life.

2. Olen Kelley _____ (miss) the combination to the safe
   the first time he tried.

3. Kelley _____ (know) the legal technicalities, but he
   sued anyway.

4. Kelley _____ (attack) several times with handguns.

5. During the interview, Kelley _____ (say) he was suing
   the distributor of Saturday Night Specials.

6. In most crimes, handguns _____ (use) to kill people.

7. Saturday Night Specials _____ (yet, exempt) from the
   proposal to lift bans against the sales of guns across state lines.

8. In Kelley's case, the robber _____ (be) a foot-and-a-half
   away from him when he shot him.

9. When Olen Kelley filed suit, he _____ (ask) for $500
   million in damages from R.G. Industries.

10. So far, Kelley _____ (take) his case to the Supreme Court.

B.   PRONUNCIATION: Rising Intonation

Notice

Listen to the following example from the interview. Notice the intonation
patterns of the underlined questions. Does the interviewer use a rising
(⌣➚) or falling (⎯➘) intonation? Draw a line to indicate the
intonation pattern that you hear.

BREEDING: <u>He shot you?</u>

KELLEY: Yes.

BREEDING: <u>Did he injure you badly?</u>

KELLEY: He shot me in the shoulder. It came out my armpit, went
back in my armpit, traveled down my side, and came out the
lower part of my side.

BREEDING: <u>How about the other times that you were attacked?</u>

<u>Were they also with guns?</u>

KELLEY: Handguns, yes.

BREEDING: <u>Who are you suing, then?</u>

Explanation   Questions usually follow a similar intonation pattern. Like the examples above, *yes/no* questions are often pronounced with a rising intonation. A rising intonation pattern is also used in statements that confirm understanding, such as in the first question above, but a rising intonation indicates to the listener that they are questions.

Wh- questions, or questions that begin with *who, what, when, where, why,* or *how* are often pronounced with a falling intonation.

Exercise

Work in pairs. Practice reading the questions with the correct intonation. Student A reads the question. Student B answers the question with information from the interview. Switch roles after item 5.

1. Do handguns account for much of the violent crime in the United States?

2. Who tried to exempt Saturday Night Specials from the proposal to lift bans across state lines?

3. Where does Olen Kelley live?

4. Has Kelley been held up more than once?

5. How many times has he been held up?

Now switch roles. A becomes B and B becomes A.

6. What were the two men after?

7. Was the money in the safe?

8. Did Kelley get shot in the shoulder?

9. Where is the gun's distributor?

10. Will Kelley take the case to the Supreme Court?

V. FOLLOW-UP ACTIVITIES

A. DISCUSSION QUESTIONS

In groups, discuss your answers to the following questions.

1. Should the sale of handguns, such as Saturday Night Specials, be banned? If so, can you think of any exceptions?

2. Do you own a gun? Would you want to own a gun? Have you ever been in a situation where you wished you had a gun to protect yourself?

B. ROLE PLAY: The Courtroom

1. Take Notes to Prepare

By focusing on important details of the Olen Kelley case and his background, you may be better able to prepare the role play that follows.

Listen to the interview again. Take notes on Olen Kelley's case. Key phrases and an example have been provided for you.

Kelley's background

• grocery store manager in Silver Spring, Maryland

_____

_____

_____

_____

The holdup

_____

_____

_____

_____

_____

_____

The suit

_____

_____

_____

_____

 2. Role Play

Work in three groups. Group A will prepare arguments for the plaintiff (Kelley).
Group B will prepare arguments for the defense (R.G. Industries). Group C will
review the facts of the case and determine courtroom conduct and procedures.
Read the situation and choose roles. Prepare for 20 minutes, then begin the
courtroom trial of _Kelley v. R.G. Industries_.

The Situation

There has been much controversy over Kelley's suit, and his case is being taken
to court. The plaintiff, Kelley, is suing a manufacturer of Saturday Night Specials,
a common handgun used in crimes. He is asking $500 million in damages. The
trial will begin shortly. In preparation for the trial, all the interested parties have
been preparing their arguments. The result of this trial will certainly have a great
impact on the future of Saturday Night Specials in particular, and national gun
laws in general.

The Roles

<u>**Group A**</u>

Kelley

Your grocery store has been held up five times. You are now suing the gun
manufacturer, who you feel is responsible for the damages. You will tell your
story to the court and give reasons why you hold the gun manufacturer
responsible. Try to imagine what the defense will say, in order to have a strong
response.

Plaintiff's Attorney

You are Kelley's attorney and will represent him in his suit for $500 million. You will present arguments as to why the gun manufacturer should be held responsible. You will also prepare your client, Kelley, to respond to the accusations and questions of the defense. Try to imagine what the defendant will say in order to have a strong argument.

Expert Witness

You are a criminal investigator. You will present data to the court indicating that an increasing number of crimes is committed with Saturday Night Specials.

Group B

R.G. Industries: Manufacturer of Saturday Night Specials

You manufacture Saturday Night Specials. You have been accused of being responsible for damages resulting from the use of the gun you manufacture. You must present arguments to defend your case.

Defendant's Attorney

You are the gun manufacturer's attorney and will represent it against the claims of the plaintiff, Kelley. You will present reasons why the gun manufacturer should not be held responsible for crimes committed with the gun. You should prepare your client, the manufacturer, to respond to the accusations and questions of the plaintiff. Try to imagine what the plaintiff will say in order to have a strong response.

Expert Witness

You are a sociologist. Present data indicating that there is no apparent correlation between crimes committed and the weapons used to commit those crimes.

Group C

The Judges

You will listen to both sides of the issue. Try to remain objective throughout the court trial. You may reject any irrelevant or "leading" questions by the attorneys. You will quietly consult with each other to decide if the attorneys' objections are to be "overruled" or "sustained." Before the trial begins, review the facts of the case with the jurors. Decide what behavior will be permitted in the courtroom. Decide on what grounds an attorney's objections will be overruled or sustained.

Note: In the American legal system, there is one judge who rules. In this role play, two judges should be used to promote discussion in the decision-making process.

The Jurors

You are six to twelve citizens who have been called to serve in court. You will listen to both sides of the issue, taking notes on relevant information. As a group, develop a system of note-taking to record the information given in court. You will use this information to make your decision on the case. You should disregard anything that the judge says is irrelevant. You will decide whether or not Kelley wins his suit. A majority vote is necessary for your decision.

Courtroom Procedure

1. The judge explains the case to the jury.

2. The plaintiff's attorney asks his or her expert witness to sit in the witness's chair. The attorney asks questions. The defendant's attorney may then ask this witness questions. An individual attorney may question a witness for no more than three minutes. Each attorney should be timed.

3. The defendant's attorney asks his or her expert witness to sit in the witness's chair. The attorney asks questions. The plaintiff's attorney may then ask this witness questions.

4. The plaintiff's attorney questions the plaintiff (Kelley). The defendant's attorney may then ask him questions.

5. The defendant's attorney questions the defendant (the gun manufacturer). The plaintiff's attorney may then ask him or her questions.

6. The defendant's attorney sums up his or her side of the case.

7. The plaintiff's attorney sums up his or her side of the case.

8. The jury deliberates in private. Jury members compare notes and discuss the details of the case. They then vote for or against the plaintiff. A majority vote rules.

9. The jury presents its decision to the court.

Useful Words and Expressions

When people speak to the judge, they say:

- Your honor.

When an attorney speaks to the judge, the attorney may say:

- Objection! (The attorney is telling the judge that the other attorney is asking questions that are not relevant to the case.)

- The plaintiff/defense rests its case. (The attorney is telling the judge that there are no more witnesses to be questioned.)

When a judge speaks to an attorney, the judge may say:

- Call your next witness. (The judge is asking the attorney to question a new witness.)

- Overruled! (The judge is telling the attorney that he/she does not agree with the attorney's objection, and therefore, the other attorney may continue asking those questions.)

- Sustained! (The judge is telling the attorney that he/she agrees with the attorney's objection, and therefore, the other attorney may not continue asking those questions.)

When a witness speaks to the attorney, the witness may say:

- I plead the Fifth.* (The witness is telling the attorney that he or she doesn't want to answer the attorney's questions. This is a legal right of the witness in the United States.)

---

* *The Fifth:* The Fifth Amendment to the U.S. Constitution excuses people from testifying against themselves in court proceedings.

"Facing the Wrong End of a Pistol" was first broadcast on *All Things Considered*, April 24, 1982. The interviewer is Leslie Breeding.

10

What Constitutes a Family?

I. ANTICIPATING THE ISSUE

A. PREDICTING

From the title, discuss what you think the report in this unit is about.

B. THINKING AHEAD

Work in groups. Read the following statements. Do you agree with them?
Does everyone in your group have the same opinion? Discuss.

1. The traditional family, in which the father works and the mother stays home to care for the children, is the ideal family.

2. Gay, or same-sex, couples should be legally recognized as a family.

3. Nontraditional families will eventually be more common than the traditional nuclear family, that is, a family made up of parents and children.

II. VOCABULARY

The words in the first column will help you understand the report. Try to guess their meaning from your knowledge of English, or use a dictionary. In each set, cross out the word that does not have a similar meaning. Then compare your answers with those of another student. Discuss the relationship between the words in each set.

1. **wage-earning**   volunteer-working   money-making   income-producing

2. **species**   type   group   member

3. **profile**   description   picture   light

4. **foster parents**   biological parents   caretakers   adoptive parents

5. **stepfamilies**   alternative families   nuclear families   nontraditional families

6. **raised**   brought up   rose   cared for

7. **seniors**   aged   elderly   middle-aged

8. **championed**   supported   defended   fought against

9. **grappling with**   ignoring   confronting   dealing with

10. **evict**   expel from   force to leave   invite to stay

11. **legitimize**   legalize   cancel   justify

12. **dependents**   guardians   children   descendants

III. LISTENING

A. TASK LISTENING

Listen to the report. Find the answer to the following question.

What are two examples of nontraditional families mentioned in the report?

B. **LISTENING FOR MAIN IDEAS**

Listen to the report again. The report has been divided into four parts. You will hear a beep at the end of each part. Answer the question for each part in a complete sentence. You should have four statements that make a summary of the report. Compare your summary with that of another student.

Part 1   What legal action has been taken in California?

_____

_____

Part 2   How does Shannon Gibson's family situation illustrate the situation of many American families today?

_____

_____

Part 3   What issue will the states be grappling with for many years?

_____

_____

Part 4   How does the family registration certificate help legal guardians such as John Brown?

_____

_____

C. **LISTENING FOR DETAILS**

Read the questions for Part 1. Then listen to Part 1 again. As you listen, circle the best answer. Compare your answers with those of another student. If you disagree, listen again.

Part 1

1. What is disappearing in the United States?

   a. a family with a working father and a mother who stays home to raise children

   b. the percentage of kids born to each family

   c. institutions that recognize alternative families

2. Which nontraditional groups are mentioned as people living together as families?

   a. same-sex partners

   b. friends sharing housing

   c. families with adopted children

Repeat the same procedure for Parts 2–4.

Part 2

3. How is Shannon Gibson like many other sixth graders?

   a. She chews gum.

   b. She has a stepmother.

   c. She doesn't live with her biological father.

4. What concern does Shannon have?

   a. Her mother will soon die.

   b. She will have to live with her biological father again.

   c. She wouldn't be able to see her stepfather someday.

5. How can a group register as a family in California?

   a. They meet with the secretary of state.

   b. They pay a $100 fee.

   c. They fill out a form.

6. Which group is *not* mentioned as one that can register with California's secretary of state as a family?

   a. stepfamilies

   b. heterosexual couples

   c. unrelated seniors

Part 3

7. What did the Family Diversity Project champion?

   a. the idea of private agencies defending the rights of the family

   b. the concept of nontraditional family registration

   c. the old concept of a family

8. What kind of court case caused the state of New York to reconsider the definition of family?

   a. eviction

   b. marriage

   c. adoption

9. Which group is *not* mentioned as a group in California that can register its name as an association?

   a. labor unions

   b. tour groups

   c. families

10. Which two states have registration procedures similar to those in California?

    a. Oregon and Washington

    b. New York and New Jersey

    c. Virginia and West Virginia

Part 4

11. How significant is the family registration certificate itself?

    a. It has important legal benefits.

    b. It has no legal benefits.

    c. It has legal benefits for fathers.

12. What role does John Brown play as a parent?

    a. He is an adoptive father.

    b. He and his wife are legal guardians.

    c. He has four dependents.

13. What does Brown say about his son?

   a. He is afraid his son won't be able to go to college.

   b. He wants to continue to claim his college-aged son as a dependent on his insurance policy.

   c. He is afraid he will lose his status as guardian for his college-aged son.

14. What is likely to happen to Brown as a result of his certificate?

   a. The Internal Revenue Service will not consider his son as a dependent.

   b. His insurance company will refuse to sell him insurance.

   c. His nontraditional family will be accepted.

D. LISTENING FOR INFERENCE

Listen to the excerpts from the report. Read the following statements. Decide whether they are true or false, based on the attitude expressed by each speaker. Write *T* or *F* next to each statement. Compare your answers with those of another student. Listen again if necessary.

Excerpt 1

_____1. Shannon feels close to Pat, her stepfather.

_____2. Shannon would rather be with her biological father than Pat, her stepfather.

_____3. Shannon is afraid she might not be able to see Pat one day.

Excerpt 2

_____4. Thomas Coleman thinks only blood relatives should be allowed to stay in a rent-controlled apartment.

_____5. Coleman thinks it's easy to distinguish a family from a non-family.

_____6. Coleman thinks it will take the courts a long time to define the rights of non-family members.

Excerpt 3

_____7. John Brown feels he has the same rights as a biological parent.

_____8. Brown is confident that the insurance company will cover his son.

_____9. Brown is expecting a fight over his family status.

IV. LOOKING AT LANGUAGE

A. USAGE: Present Unreal Conditional

Notice   Listen to the following example from the interview. Notice the boldfaced verb form in the statements. What situation is the speaker reacting to? Is she talking about the present or the past?

> Pat is not my biological father, but he's raised me since I was two years old. So, it **wouldn't be** right . . . that I *wouldn't be able* to see him or anything like that.

Explanation   In the statement above, the speaker is reacting to an unreal situation in the present. She imagines an unreal result of an unreal condition. Although she does not say this, the following conditions are implied:

> (If my stepfather didn't get visitation rights, . . .) it **wouldn't be** right . . .

The present unreal conditional is generally formed as follows:

Condition clause	Result clause
If + subject + past tense	subject + *would* + *base verb*
If my stepfather didn't get visitation rights,	**it wouldn't be** right . . .

Exercise

Complete the sentences, expressing ideas about traditional and nontraditional families in your culture. Use the present unreal pattern in each sentence.

1. If a child had a biological father and a stepfather, <u>she would/wouldn't be able to</u> <u>spend time with both of them.</u>

2. If someone made a profile of traditional families in my country, _____

   _____

3. If gay couples or unrelated seniors wanted to be recognized officially as families

in my country, _____

_____

4. _____

people's reactions would be very different.

5. If I were asked what constitutes a family, _____

_____

6. _____

the nuclear family would become less important.

B. PRONUNCIATION: Suffix Pronunciation in Different Word Forms

Notice > Listen to the following example from the report. Focus on the boldfaced verb. Would the pronunciation of this word change if it were used as a noun?

The U.S. Census Bureau ***estimates*** that just 15 percent of American families fit this profile.

Explanation > Many English verbs end with the suffix -*ate*. The pronunciation of the suffix in the verb form is: /eyt/. The verb above is pronounced: /ɛstəmeyts/.

Many of these verbs have noun or adjective word forms. The pronunciation of the suffix changes, however, when the word is used as a noun or adjective. As a noun, the word *estimates* is pronounced: /ɛstəmɪts/.

Exercise

Work with a partner. Take turns reading the following sentences aloud. Use the correct suffix pronunciation based on the word's usage.

1. a. Shannon's two fathers must **coordinate** to schedule weekends with Shannon.

   b. Shannon's sixth-grade teacher is having her students study the **coordinates** on the globe.

2. a. Shannon's biological father and stepfather see Shannon on **alternate** weekends.

   b. Shannon **alternates** weekends with her biological father and her stepfather.

3. a. In the near future, the states will have to **elaborate** on their definition of "family."

   b. On the TV show *The Golden Girls*, the women don't cook **elaborate** dinners for themselves because they don't have a lot of money.

4. a. Since unrelated seniors are considered **associates** living together in a group, they qualify as a family.

   b. Shannon's mother and stepfather registered as a family so that her stepfather would be able to **associate** with Shannon if her mother died.

5. a. The traditional **moderate**-income family with a wage-earning father and a wife who stays home to take care of the kids is disappearing in the United States.

   b. Unrelated seniors share housing like a family in order to **moderate** their living expenses.

6. a. Registering non-traditional groups as family **correlates** with economic living situations.

   b. Shannon's relationship with her stepfather is the **correlate** of her relationship with her biological father because she cares about them equally.

7. a. John Brown gave an **estimate** of his taxes, claiming his four teenage boys as dependents.

   b. In the New York Court of Appeals housing survivor case, the court had to **estimate** what qualifies as "family."

8. a. It is always difficult for children when their parents ***separate*** or divorce.

    b. Shannon's life with her biological father is ***separate*** from her life with her mother and stepfather.

9. a. The child welfare committee had to ***deliberate*** for a long time before deciding whether or not the couple could qualify as foster parents.

    b. John Brown made a ***deliberate*** decision to claim his four sons as dependents.

10. a. John Brown is a strong ***advocate*** for the rights of his sons as dependents.

    b. John Brown will ***advocate*** for insurance coverage for his son who will go to college next year.

V. FOLLOW-UP ACTIVITIES

A. DISCUSSION QUESTIONS

In groups, discuss your answers to the following questions.

1. Why, in your opinion, is the traditional family disappearing in the United States?

2. What is your reaction to California's public registration of nontraditional families?

3. Would you become a member of a nontraditional family? If so, under what circumstances?

B.   SURVEY: What Constitutes a Family?

1. Take Notes to Prepare

Although California has officially recognized nontraditional groups as families, not everyone would agree with California's definition of family, that is, any group of people living together. By taking notes on the specific groups mentioned in the report and on their reasons for registering as families, you may be better able to interpret public opinion in the survey that follows.

Listen to the report again. Take notes on California's new registration policy for nontraditional families. Key phrases and an example have been provided for you. Use your notes to help you formulate questions for the survey that follows.

Examples of nontraditional families

• _gay couples_ _____

_____

_____

_____

_____

_____

Reasons nontraditional families want to register as a family

_____

_____

_____

_____

2. Survey

Work in a group of four or five students. Write a questionnaire with five yes/no questions that ask people's opinions about what constitutes a family. Your group will interview a variety of people. Decide where and when you will conduct the survey, how many people you will question, who they will be, and so on.

Conduct your survey. Then tally the *yes* and *no* responses and note any significant comments that people made. The following chart can be used to record your questions, tally responses, and record comments. An example has been provided.

Questions	Yes	No	Comments
Do gay couples qualify as a family?	///	//	They have the same rights as heterosexual couples.

Oral Report

When your group meets again, summarize the information you've gathered in your survey. Prepare an oral report to present to the rest of the class. Be sure to include an introduction to your survey, a summary of the results you've gathered, and a conclusion including your own interpretation of your findings.

Oral Presentation Procedures

1. The first student introduces the group and gives an introduction to the survey that was conducted.

2. The next few students present one or two of the questions that were asked, statistics or general responses that were received, and interesting comments that were made by the people who were interviewed. The comments mentioned should help explain why people answered the way they did.

3. The last student concludes the presentation by summarizing the findings from the survey, interpreting them, and perhaps reacting to the results. For example, "We were surprised to learn that most people thought . . ."

Useful Words and Phrases

When you talk about the people who answered your survey, you can call them:

- interviewees
- respondents

When you report the information you gathered, you can begin:

- They agreed that . . .
- They felt that . . .
- They believed that . . .
- They stated that . . .

When you indicate the number of people surveyed, you can say:

- More than half agreed that . . .
- Over 50 percent of the sample stated that . . .
- Less than a third said that . . .

"What Constitutes a Family?" was first broadcast on *Weekend All Things Considered*, December 15, 1990. The reporter is Kitty Felde.

Business Across Borders:
Is Bigger Necessarily Better?

Robert Eaton and Jürgen Schrempp were co-chairs of German-American automaker DaimlerChrysler at the time Daimler-Benz AG and Chrysler merged. Mr. Eaton retired in 2000.

I. ANTICIPATING THE ISSUE

A. PREDICTING

From the title, discuss what you think the interview in this unit is about.

B. THINKING AHEAD

In groups, discuss your answers to the following questions.

1. Why are more and more companies joining across borders? What advantages are there to international mergers?

2. What kinds of problems might happen when companies from different countries join together?

3. How might international mergers affect the role of governments?

II. ▷ VOCABULARY

The words in the first column will help you understand the interview. Try to guess their meaning from your knowledge of English, or use a dictionary. In each set, cross out the word that does not have a similar meaning. Then compare your answers with those of another student. Discuss the relationship between the words in each set.

1.	**scale**	size	picture	amount
2.	**watershed**	critical point	historic change	forgotten story
3.	**takeover**	merger	buyout	change in control
4.	**spurred**	stopped	stimulated	encouraged
5.	**consolidating**	joining	separating	integrating
6.	**regulatory**	controlling	having many rules	open
7.	**reconcile**	argue	bring together	resolve
8.	**gravitating**	moving toward	feeling sick	being attracted to
9.	**resurgence**	remark	rebirth	reappearance
10.	**eclipse**	loss of fame	loss of memory	loss of power

III. ▷ LISTENING

A. TASK LISTENING

Listen to the interview. Find the answer to the following question.

Which car companies are mentioned as examples of companies that may have to consolidate in the future?*

*At the time of the interview, the companies mentioned were all independent. They have since formed partnerships with other car companies.

B. **LISTENING FOR MAIN IDEAS**

Listen to the interview again. The interview has been divided into six parts. You will hear a beep at the end of each part. Choose the best answer for each question. Compare your answers with those of another student. Try to agree on the answers.

Part 1   What is becoming more common, as illustrated by Daimler-Chrysler?

    a. the merging of companies internationally

    b. the merging of German and American companies

    c. the merging of companies culturally

Part 2   What significance does the Daimler-Chrysler merger have regarding international mergers?

    a. American companies will take over more foreign companies.

    b. Foreign companies will take over more American companies.

    c. American companies and foreign companies will stop joining forces.

Part 3   How easy is it to implement cross-border mergers?

    a. There are a number of problems.

    b. It depends on the companies that want to merge.

    c. They are becoming easier and easier with globalization.

Part 4   What impact will the Daimler-Chrysler merger have on other auto industries?

    a. It will prevent future mergers in the auto industry.

    b. It will cause smaller companies to go out of business.

    c. It will force smaller companies to consolidate.

Part 5   What reaction will countries have to the Daimler-Chrysler merger?

    a. Regulatory issues will have to be worked out.

    b. Environmental standards will have to be strengthened.

    c. Trade policies will become less protectionist.

Part 6   What role will governments play with international mergers?

  a. Governments will become less involved.

  b. Governments will become more involved.

  c. Governments will consolidate.

C. LISTENING FOR DETAILS

Read the statements for Part 1. Then listen to Part 1 again and decide whether the statements are true or false. As you listen, write *T* or *F* next to each statement. Compare your answers with those of another student. If you disagree, listen again.

Part 1

_____ 1. Government and business leaders are examining the Daimler-Chrysler merger.

_____ 2. The scale of the deal is not unusual.

_____ 3. National boundaries are no longer a problem for company expansion.

Repeat the same procedure for Parts 2–6.

Part 2

_____ 4. The Daimler-Chrysler merger was the biggest industrial merger ever.

_____ 5. According to Jeffrey Garten, it's a watershed.

_____ 6. The Daimler-Chrysler merger marks the beginning of a new trend.

Part 3

_____ 7. This merger will likely spur more global integration of the biggest companies.

_____ 8. Cultural differences are a big concern with international mergers.

_____ 9. Operational differences are not a problem because companies operate similarly.

_____ 10. International mergers are easier in practice than they seem on paper.

Part 4

_____ 11. In the future, there will be more mergers in the auto industry specifically.

_____ 12. The smaller firms in the automobile industry have been consolidating.

_____ 13. Competition will force companies to become bigger.

_____ 14. Renault, Peugeot, and Mazda formed a partnership.

Part 5

_____ 15. Anti-trust* issues will be an important consideration with global mergers.

_____ 16. The SEC (Securities and Exchange Commission) will need to approve the financial arrangements between companies that merge internationally.

_____ 17. Mercedes has always met American car industry standards.

_____ 18. Chrysler is more protectionist than Mercedes.

Part 6

_____ 19. There has been an eclipse of national governments as the center of international power.

_____ 20. Governments have different procedures and laws for global mergers than companies have.

_____ 21. Governments are able to join across borders more easily than companies.

*_Anti-trust:_ preventing companies from unfairly controlling prices

D. LISTENING FOR INFERENCE

Listen to the excerpts from the interview. For each excerpt, put a check (✔) by the statement(s) reflecting the view expressed by the speaker(s).

Excerpt 1

_____ 1. The significance of the Daimler-Chrysler merger is clear to government and business leaders.

_____ 2. This merger was not the first merger between companies in two geographically distant countries.

Excerpt 2

_____ 3. There are more international mergers in the auto industry than in other industries.

_____ 4. Smaller car companies will have a hard time competing with merged companies.

Excerpt 3

_____ 5. In the end, governments will have no control of mergers.

_____ 6. Governments are more conservative than businesses.

IV. LOOKING AT LANGUAGE

A. USAGE: Expressing Partial Agreement or Reservation

Notice   Listen to the following examples from the interview. Focus on the expressions used by Jeffrey Garten to indicate that he does not completely agree with the ideas in the interviewer's questions. Underline those expressions.

Examples

1. BOB EDWARDS: So, it'll spur more global integration with the biggest companies here in the U.S. and Europe and Asia joining forces?

   JEFFREY GARTEN: I think—I think it's likely to. But I also think it will—it will make very clear that these are going to be very difficult transactions to work out in the end. There are a huge number of problems.

2. BOB EDWARDS: What about anti-trust considerations? Any reason for the U.S. and European regulators to stand in the way of this Daimler-Chrysler merger?

   JEFFREY GARTEN: Well, I don't think it will be an anti-trust issue per se. But there are a lot of big regulatory questions that are going to arise.

3. BOB EDWARDS: So the governments are just reacting to the agenda set by business?

   JEFFREY GARTEN: Yes. But, you know, at some point here you will see, I believe, a resurgence of government intervention. Because the issues that I mentioned—SEC, environment— there are going to be some labor issues, issues relating to trade policies . . . this will bring government into the fore.

Explanation

In each of the above examples, Jeffrey Garten acknowledges the viewpoint of the interviewer, but he indicates that there is more information to better understand the issue. These forms of partial agreement are helpful in keeping a conversation going. They are also helpful for disagreeing politely.

The box on page 153 has some common expressions to show partial agreement or polite disagreement.

Yes, but . . .	I can see what you mean, but . . .
That's an interesting point, but . . .	I can see what you're getting at . . .
You have a point, but . . .	Yes, that may be true, but . . .
I agree with you to a certain extent, but . . .	Well, you may be right, but . . .
I understand what you're saying, but . . .	

Exercise

Work in pairs to practice showing partial agreement or reservation. Student A reads the first strong position on international mergers. Student B shows partial agreement or reservation. Use one of the expressions from the box above. Student A responds to Student B's opinion, showing partial agreement or reservation. Use one of the expressions from the box above.

Example Position

Student A	**Student B**	**Student A**
The Daimler-Chrysler merger is a watershed in the process of globalization.	**Well, you may be right, but** some companies may not want to consolidate because of regulatory issues.	**That's an interesting point, but** only the big companies will be able to compete in the future.

1. **Position 1**

   The cultural differences between companies from different countries will make international mergers almost impossible!

2. **Position 2**

   There will be more global integration among the biggest companies in the U.S., Europe, and Asia.

3. **Position 3**

   Cross border mergers have more problems than benefits.

Now switch roles. Student B will read the position, Student A will show partial agreement or reservation, and Student B will respond to Student A's opinion.

4. **Position 4**

   All the smaller car makers will be forced to consolidate now!

5. **Position 5**

   I think countries will become more regulatory because of these global mergers.

6. **Position 6**

   With cross-border mergers, national governments will lose their power to regulate businesses.

B.   PRONUNCIATION: Stress Changes in Words with Suffixes

Notice   Listen to the following examples from the interview. Mark the stressed syllable in each of the boldfaced words. Then, work with a partner to think of other forms of the word. How does the stress change in those forms?

1. The scale of the deal is unusual, but what's becoming more commonplace is the joining of companies that are *geographically* distant and perhaps culturally distinct.

2. There have been very few foreign takeovers of major American *industrial* companies, and I think this will set a mark and perhaps accentuate that kind of trend.

3. So it'll spur more global *integration*, with the biggest companies here in the U.S. and Europe and Asia joining forces?

Explanation   Most words with suffixes do not change their stress pattern in English (for example, *culturally* in Example 1).

However, when the suffixes *–ically*, *-ial*, and *-tion* are added to base words, as in the boldfaced words on page 154, the stressed syllable changes require a stress change from the base words. In each case, the syllable before the suffix receives the stress. Read the word pairs aloud. Listen to the shift in stress from the base word:

1. geography   geographically

2. industry   industrial

3. integrate   integration

Other suffixes that require the same shift in syllable stress are:

-sion, -ic, -ical, -ity ,-ian, -graphy, -logy, or *-tional*

Exercise

The boldfaced words below were used in the interview. Listen to the audio and mark the stressed syllable for each word and for each of its word forms. Notice whether or not there is a shift in stress.

1. **operate**   operation   operational

2. **global**   globalize   globalization

3. **continue**   continual   continuation

4. **implement**   implemented   implementation

5. **consolidate**   consolidated   consolidation

6. **notice**   notify   notification

7. **environment**   environmental   environmentally

8. **reconcile**   reconciled   reconciliation   reconciliatory

9. **gravitate**   gravitated   gravitation   gravitational

V.   FOLLOW-UP ACTIVITIES

A.   DISCUSSION QUESTIONS

In groups, discuss your answers to the following questions.

1. What kinds of cultural issues should be addressed to make a cross-border merger a success?

2. Many people believe that as political boundaries continue to come down, cultural differences will become even more pronounced because people will hold on more strongly to their own identities. Do you agree or disagree with this prediction? Give examples to support your views.

B.   SIMULATION GAME: The Daimler-Chrysler Merger

 1. Take Notes to Prepare

By focusing on the issues related to cross-border mergers that were raised by Jeffrey Garten, you may be better able to play the roles in the simulation that follows.

Listen to the interview again. Take notes on the Daimler-Chrysler merger described in the interview. Key phrases and an example have been provided for you.

Role Daimler-Chrysler merger will play in the world

• *companies will see national boundaries as no obstacle to their expansion*

_____

_____

Problems with cross-border mergers

_____

_____

_____

_____

Government roles in cross-border mergers

_____

_____

_____

_____

✔ 2. Simulation

Work in small groups.   You are a group of top Daimler-Chrysler managers who have been asked to help integrate the American and German cultural styles in the company.

Read the situation and the list of differences in management styles in the company. Which management styles will most benefit the merged international company? Make a list of policies that should be used in cross-cultural training workshops for all Daimler-Chrysler managers.

The Situation

Since the Daimler-Chrysler merger, it has become clear that the company has serious problems. The promised cost savings have not been realized. The so-called "merger" has begun to look more like a German takeover of an American company. Most importantly, the German and American styles of management differ significantly, and this culture clash has prevented the company from using its combined strengths. Daimler-Benz managers are used to producing quality cars, whereas Chrysler managers are used to producing cost-effective cars. The two groups of managers have different cultural attitudes and customs. Cooperation has been difficult, even on the simplest matters.

In theory, the Daimler-Chrysler merger makes sense. On the other hand, cultural differences could cause negative effects for the company. The CEO of Daimler-Chrysler has requested that clear managerial policies be established and that managers from each side of Daimler-Chrysler receive cross-cultural training. The established managerial policies for the merged company will be the basis for that training.

Differences in Management Styles

Daimler-Benz Managers (Germany)	Chrysler Managers (The United States)
• make careful decisions; check everything with experts	• make fast decisions; correct mistakes as they go
• focus on precision and details	• focus on big concepts and efficiency
• dislike huge pay differences	• accustomed to different salaries
• produce lengthy reports	• produce little paperwork
• have extended discussions	• prefer short meetings and quick decisions
• like planning	• like trial-and-error experimentation
• use top-down management; have respect for authority	• use consensus management; easily point out problems to superiors
• have formal dress codes and manners (jackets; handshakes)	• have casual dress codes and manners (no jackets; "How are ya?")
• speak several languages	• don't usually speak languages other than English
• address co-workers formally	• use first names to address co-workers

"Business Across Borders: Is Bigger Necessarily Better?" was first broadcast on *Morning Edition*, May 8, 1998. The interviewer is Bob Edwards.

12

Green Consumerism

A. PREDICTING

From the title, discuss what you think the interview in this unit is about.

B. THINKING AHEAD

In groups, discuss your answers to the following questions.

1. Have you made any changes in your daily life that reflect a concern for the environment? If so, what are they?

2. How much of an impact has the environmental movement had on your country? How does it compare with what's happening in other countries?

3. False advertising is when a company does not tell the truth about their product or service. Have you seen any examples of false advertising for protecting the environment? If so, give examples.

II. VOCABULARY

Read the text. The boldfaced words will help you understand the interview. Try to determine the meaning of these words. Write the number of each word next to its definition or synonym in the list at the end of the text.

In recent decades we have become more aware of all the problems that humans have created for the earth. Ozone **depletion**, acid rain, the greenhouse effect, and deforestation are only some of the environmental issues that were unknown to most people three decades ago.

With all these environmental problems, people have begun to look for ways to save the earth. Consciousness-raising groups, whose work is to get all of us to realize that we have a part to play in helping to save the planet, have been formed. Even small changes in the way we live can help to save the earth. For example, many families now turn food waste into **compost** rather than throw it away as garbage. Compost can then be put back into the soil to help gardens grow.

Yet environmental **watchdogs** tell us that we must be careful not to **jump** too quickly **on the bandwagon**. One **pitfall** to contributing in small ways to help save the environment is that we may feel a false sense of **complacency**. How many of us end up feeling good and satisfied that we have helped save the earth after only recycling our cans, bottles, and newspapers, for example? The real tasks in saving the planet are much greater than just recycling.

Another problem environmentalists point out is false advertising. Just because a product claims that it is "environmentally safe" does not mean that using it is really good for the environment. They point out that, even in the area of environmental protection, there are dishonest people trying to make a profit out of a good cause: Hucksters exist in all areas of life. We must be **leery** of the **rhetoric** of those people who falsely advertise or claim environmental concern where it doesn't exist. In the area of green consumerism, this is especially important. For example, Texaco has offered its customers a free tree seedling for the purchase of gas. This is an interesting advertising **strategy** by Texaco. The message here is that if you plant a tree, you will help make the earth a greener place. But, of course, the gas we buy from Texaco will continue to harm the earth.

We need to start convincing corporations to change their policies, to work at **_revitalizing_** our transportation systems, and generally to think about just
10
consuming less of everything—if we're really going to make a difference.

_____ a. set of plans to achieve success

_____ b. making something strong and powerful again

_____ c. natural fertilizer

_____ d. language used to persuade or influence people

_____ e. reduction

_____ f. join what seems to be successful

_____ g. danger

_____ h. self-satisfaction

_____ i. people who make sure that other people follow rules

_____ j. suspicious; wary

III. LISTENING

A. TASK LISTENING

Listen to the interview. You will hear some examples of absurd advertising. As you listen, draw lines to connect each product with its false advertising promise.

Product	False Advertising Promise
gasoline	is good breakfast cereal
car	makes the world a greener place
candy	encourages new values

B. LISTENING FOR MAIN IDEAS

Listen to the interview again. The interview has been divided into five parts. You will hear a beep at the end of each part. A word or phrase has been given to help you focus on the main idea of each part. Write the main idea in a complete sentence. You should have five statements that make a summary of the interview. Compare your summary with that of another student.

Part 1   false complacency

_____

_____

Part 2   shopping

_____

_____

Part 3   longer-term issue

_____

_____

Part 4   green marketing

_____

_____

Part 5   revitalizing

_____

_____

C. LISTENING FOR DETAILS

Read the questions for Part 1. Then listen to Part 1 again. As you listen, circle the best answer. Compare your answers with those of another student. If you disagree, listen again.

Part 1

1. Which of these book titles is *not* mentioned in the introduction to the interview?

   a. *The Green Consumer*

   b. *Shopping for a Better World*

   c. *Fifteen Simple Things You Can Do to Save the Planet*

2. What general purpose do these books have?

   a. to broaden the environmental movement

   b. to make our ordinary lives more complete

   c. to lull consumers into a false complacency

3. What do Alan Durning and Alice Tepper Marlin have in common?

   a. They are both researchers at the World Watch Institute.

   b. They are both members of the Council on Economic Priorities.

   c. They are both authors of the book *Shopping for a Better World.*

Repeat the same procedure for Parts 2–5.

Part 2

4. What one thing does Alice Tepper Marlin feel we can do to help the environment?

   a. consume less

   b. grow better foods

   c. throw away the compost heap

5. What should we do when we shop?

 a. not use shopping carts

 b. change the places where we shop

 c. look at product contents

Part 3

6. Which comment does Alan Durning *not* make about the advice on shopping?

 a. It's a really great idea.

 b. It's a first step.

 c. It's a good long-term plan.

7. Who is responsible for over consumption, according to Durning?

 a. one hundred billion people in nonindustrial countries

 b. people living in advanced countries

 c. the majority of the world's population

8. Which of the earth's environmental problems is *not* mentioned?

 a. greenhouse effect

 b. acid rain

 c. deforestation

9. What specific solution does Durning propose?

 a. We need to consume our way out of this.

 b. We have to shift our emphasis to gross consumption.

 c. We have to simplify our lifestyles.

Part 4

10. How does Durning see green consuming?

 a. It's like taking a trip on the Titanic.*

 b. He thinks it's an initial educational step.

 c. He is critical of it.

 * *Titanic:* A passenger ship that sank and in which many people died.

11. Where do we see a lot of "greenwash" going on?

    a. in corporate advertising

    b. at tree farms

    c. in supermarkets

12. Which of the following areas is *not* mentioned as an area where we can find hucksters?

    a. in health clubs

    b. in food marketing

    c. in green consumerism

13. How does Tepper Marlin suggest we deal with hucksters?

    a. We need to throw out the entire concept of green consumerism.

    b. Consumers need to listen to hucksters.

    c. Federal guidelines need to be established.

Part 5

14. What negative result could occur from the green-consuming movement?

    a. People won't feel good.

    b. Yuppies* will stop recycling bottles and newspapers.

    c. People won't do as much as they need to do.

15. What example does Toyota use for green advertising?

    a. Their cars have a new series of valves.

    b. Their cars don't need excess gas.

    c. People who drive their cars have the right values.

16. What does Durning think we need to focus on?

    a. reforming transportation

    b. limiting public transportation

    c. controlling rail transportation

Yuppies: Young urban professionals; yuppies has also taken on a negative sense in referring to young people who focus a great deal on material wealth.

17. What happened in the 1980s, according to Durning?

    a. We didn't reach the people who wanted to help.

    b. We focused too much on little things.

    c. We began to make a difference.

D. LISTENING FOR INFERENCE

Listen to the excerpts from the interview. Try to understand the speaker's meaning by listening to his or her tone of voice and choice of words. Choose the best answer for each question. Compare your answers with those of another student. Listen to the excerpts again if necessary.

Excerpt 1

1. Which of the following *best* describes Durning's attitude toward Tepper Marlin's suggestions?

    a. He thinks they are a great idea.

    b. He thinks they are useful, but not the complete answer.

    c. He thinks they won't work very well.

Excerpt 2

2. Why does the interviewer, Steve Curwood, compare green consuming to the Titanic?

    a. Green consuming will lead to a disaster in the environment.

    b. Green consuming will have a big impact on the environment.

    c. Green consuming only helps the environment on the surface.

Excerpt 3

3. What does Durning think about Toyota's ads?

    a. He doesn't believe they are honest.

    b. He thinks they focus excessively on recycling.

    c. He admires their focus on friends and community.

IV. LOOKING AT LANGUAGE

A. USAGE: Causative Verbs

Notice

Listen to the following example from the interview. Notice the boldfaced verb. What is the meaning of the verb in this sentence? What is the form of the verb that follows it?

There's a definite risk that this will ***make*** us feel better than we really are. But it's a risk that we have to take.

Explanation

Causative verbs are used to show that someone or something causes others to do something. *Make, have,* and *get* are causative verbs.

These verbs are formed as follows:

Base form

make or *have* + someone
+ *do* something

(EXAMPLE: ***make*** or ***have***
the government ***pass*** laws)

Infinitive form

get + someone + *to do*
something

(EXAMPLE: ***get*** the senators   +
to pass laws)

VERB	EXAMPLE	MEANING
Make	Justin's parents **make** him **take out** the compost each week.	*Make* expresses force or pressure.
Have	The mayor should **have** the sanitation workers **recycle** garbage more frequently.	*Have* is used in situations of authority.
Get	The public should **get** the government **to pass** regulations to protect the environment.	*Get* expresses persuasion.

Two of the causative verbs can be used in passive voice: *have* and *get*. Both *have* and *get* are followed by the past participle in passive sentences as in the following examples:

The senators **had** environmental regulations **passed**.

The public **got** environmental regulations **passed**.

Exercise

There are many things we can do at home, school, or work to save the earth. Use the following cues to form complete sentences with *have*, *make*, or *get* to express your own ideas about how we can influence others to help save the earth. Use active sentences in 1–6 and passive sentences in 7–10.

1. our family / consume

   We can get our families to consume less energy at home.

   _____

2. the government / pass laws

   _____

   _____

3. our community / change

   _____

   _____

4. our friends / take important steps

   _____

   _____

5. our supermarkets / sell

   _____

   _____

6. our politicians / consider

_____

_____

7. trees / plant

_____

_____

8. transportation systems / revitalize

_____

_____

9. products / label

_____

_____

10. advertising / control

_____

_____

B. **PRONUNCIATION: Words with Silent Consonants**

Notice

Listen to the following example from the interview. One word has a silent letter—a letter which is not pronounced—in it. Underline the silent letter.

We have got to shift our emphasis away from gross consumption of things to a more, maybe, subtle lifestyle.

Explanation

More than 60 percent of English words contain silent letters. It is useful to memorize common words with silent letters. Since their pronunciation and spellings are different from each other, it is easy to make mistakes in both speaking and writing.

In the example, the word *subtle* has a silent *b* before the *t*. Other words with a silent *b* in a *bt* combination are *debt* and *doubt*.

Exercise

Work with a partner. Take turns reading the following words aloud. In each word, underline the letter which is *not* pronounced. Write the words in the chart next to the rules they follow.

bought	psychology	taught
knife	condemn	scissors
rhythm	knee	thought
~~climb~~	scene	tomb
lamb	knock	wring
night	science	wrist
comb	psychiatry	straight
ought	wrong	
know	rhyme	

SILENT LETTERS	EXAMPLES
Silent *b* in *mb* at the end of a word	*climb*
Silent *c* in *sc* at the beginning of a word	
Silent *k* in *kn*	
Silent *n* in *mn* at the end of a word	
Silent *p* in *ps* at the beginning of a word	
Silent *gh* in *ght*	
Silent *h* after the letter *r*	
Silent *w* in the *wr* at the beginning of a word	

V. FOLLOW-UP ACTIVITIES

A. DISCUSSION QUESTIONS

In groups, discuss your answers to the following questions.

1. Do you believe that green consuming is a "vehicle for raising people's consciousness"? Does green consumerism really help people contribute to saving the earth? Why or why not?

2. Alan Durning states that "we at the top are the problem." Do you agree that industrialized countries have more of a responsibility toward saving the earth than developing countries do? Why or why not?

B. VALUES CLARIFICATION: To Save the Earth

1. Take Notes to Prepare

By focusing on the suggestions made in the interview and whether they are seen as important for saving the environment, you may be better able to clarify your values in the exercise that follows.

Listen to the interview again. Take notes on the practical suggestions that are given for protecting the environment. Key areas of concern have been provided for you. Write the suggestions that relate to each concern. In the right-hand column, indicate whether the interviewees express a positive (+) or negative (-) view of the suggestion. Use your notes to help you in the values clarification exercise that follows.

	Practical Suggestions for Saving the Environment	+ or -
Consumption	• we should consume less	+

	Practical Suggestions for Saving the Environment	**+ or -**
Planting the earth	_____	_____
	_____	_____
	_____	_____
Education and public policy	_____	_____
	_____	_____
	_____	_____
	_____	_____
	_____	_____
	_____	_____
Recycling	_____	_____
	_____	_____
Transportation	_____	_____
	_____	_____
	_____	_____
	_____	_____

2. Values Clarification

In the 1990s, a book was published to help people get involved in protecting the environment. *50 Simple Things You Can Do to Save the Earth* quickly became a national bestseller. Similar publications followed, including *100 Ways You Can Save the World* and *101 Ways to Heal the Earth*.

Work in groups. Read the following list of 30 recommendations from books about saving the earth. Then categorize them into the five general areas of concern listed above: consumption, planting the earth, education and public policy, recycling, and transportation.

After you have categorized the items, rank each of the areas of concern in order from the most important (1) to the least important (5) ways to "save the earth." Try to reach a group consensus. Present your categories and ranking to the class.

1. Buy plain white toilet paper, tissues, and paper towels. Dyed paper pollutes.

2. Walk or ride a bike instead of using the car for short trips.

3. Keep your car tires inflated to the proper pressure to improve fuel economy.

4. Turn off lights in rooms you aren't using.

5. Plant trees. This can reduce heating and cooling bills, help prevent soil erosion, and reduce air pollution.

6. Investigate the environmental record of companies you invest in. Write a letter as a shareholder to the company president, or sell your stock.

7. Recycle all cans and bottles.

8. Share rides to work, or use public transportation.

9. Buy a fuel-efficient car, one which gets a minimum of 35 miles per gallon.

10. Read labels and research the products you buy.

11. Buy products packaged in recycled paper or cardboard.

12. Limit your use of "disposable" items.

13. Close off unused areas of your home. Shut off or block heat vents.

14. Compare energy-guide labels when buying appliances.

15. Tune up your car regularly for maximum gas mileage.

16. Learn about global climate change.

17. Rent or borrow items you don't often use. Efficient use of products conserves resources.

18. Avoid products made from tropical-rainforest woods.

19. Instead of toxic mothballs, buy cedar chips.

20. Don't litter. Pick up any garbage you see, especially plastic rings that can trap birds and fish.

21. Join an environmental organization.

22. Buy recycled paper products, stationery, and greeting cards.

23. Shop at your local farmers' market. Products are fresh, packaging is minimal, and foods are less likely to be contaminated with preservatives and pesticides.

24. Start an organic garden.

25. Buy in bulk to avoid overpackaging.

26. Avoid optional equipment on cars that decreases fuel economy.

27. Urge your community to start a recycling program.

28. Start a recycling program where you work.

29. Give leftover paint to theater groups, schools, or church groups.

30. Educate your children about the environment.

Excerpted from *Iowa Energy Bulletin's* list of "100 Ways You Can Save the Earth"

"Green Consumerism" was first broadcast on *Living on Earth*, May 3, 1991. The interviewer is Steve Curwood.